Hammer.
Nail.
Wood.

Hammer.
Nail.
Wood.

The Compulsion
to Build.

BY

THOMAS GLYNN

ILLUSTRATIONS BY VANCE SMITH

CHELSEA GREEN PUBLISHING COMPANY
White River Junction, Vermont
Totnes, England

Designed by Dede Cummings

Printed in the United States of America
First printing March 1998
01 00 99   2 3 4 5

Library of Congress Cataloging-in-Publication Data
Glynn, Thomas, 1935–
    Hammer—nail—wood : the compulsion to build/by Thomas Glynn:
  illustrations by Vance Smith.
       p.   cm.
     ISBN 1–890132–06–3 (alk. paper)
     1. Log cabins—New York—Design and construction—Ancedotes.
  2. Glynn, Thomas, 1935–   —Anecdotes. 3. Country life—New York—
  Anecdotes. 4. Saint Lawrence River Valley—Social life and customs.
  I. Title
    TH4840.G58   1998
  690'.837—dc21   97–51576

CHELSEA GREEN PUBLISHING COMPANY
P.O. BOX 428
WHITE RIVER JUNCTION, VERMONT
(800) 639-4099
WWW: CHELSEAGREEN.COM

This book is dedicated to Eldon and Donald Wells, brothers and farmers. They are gone but they are not forgotten.

My home over there, my home over there,
My home over there, now I remember it!
And when I see that mountain far away,
Why, then I weep. Alas! What can I do?
What can I do? Alas! What can I do?
My home over there, now I remember it.

Tewa song

Contents

Contents

Contents

Acknowledgments

This house would not have been built without the help of many people. Foremost were Clyde Morse and Nick Gardinier, without whom the actual building would never have been done. Some of the stories are mine alone, and some that Clyde told me I have taken the liberty of changing. Mose Miller and his brother Dan helped me with the deck and assembling the bents, and also supplied the humor, deflating my ego on occasion. Paul Simmons and his father were responsible for drilling the well. I learned the art & science of post-and-beam construction at the Shelter Institute in Bath, Maine. I give special thanks to Pat and Patsy Hennin and their son Raoul, who were kind, patient, and precise. Needless to say, any mistakes or changes I have made in building are mine and not theirs. Spindle Corey, Bonnie Gardinier, and many others in the North Country community and Brooklyn, I thank you. Thanks also to the New York Foundation for the Arts for their support.

Finally, and most importantly, to Patricia, my helpmate, my soulmate, my love, who supported me most when I needed it and who was willing, still is, to take a chance on a dream.

Hammer.
Nail.
Wood.

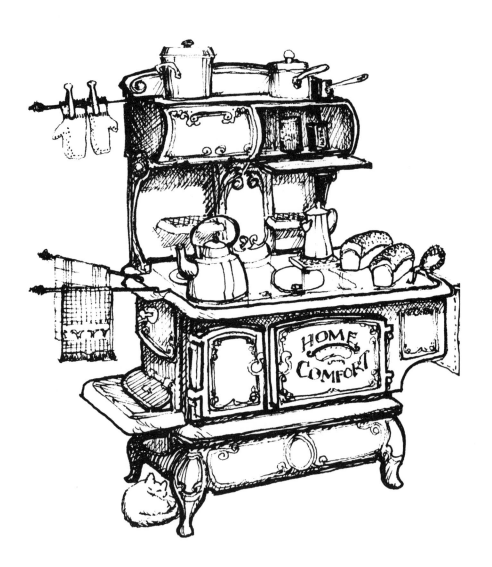

One hundred and thirty acres. Far away.

IT WAS CHEAP LAND because it was far from the city, far away in northern New York near the St. Lawrence River. The closest big city was in Canada, an hour and a half away. My wife and I bought it because I grew up in the city and dreamed of living on a farm, being totally ignorant of farms. I didn't really want to live on a farm, I wanted to live on the idea of a farm. This was an old broken-down farm, pasture and meadows, a sad house beautiful in its lines but poked through by the weather with a tiny spring that ran haphazardly through the basement. The barn leaned to one side so precariously it was cabled to the slant of the hill it rested on, the cables spiked to the ground, clutching huge boulders. They held not just the one side but passed through to the other side. The foundation had cracked and was slowly sliding downhill, leaving the barn unsure of where it wanted to be. Pigeons nested in the hayloft and took the morning air on the shingled roof through an opening they had made. Every year we came up for several weeks during the summer and pawed through the house to see what had changed and guessed how much more the barn had tilted. We chased the

Hammer. Nail. Wood.

mice out and I borrowed a rifle to shoot a mole that was eating the roots of a fruit tree in the front yard. I never fired a shot. Then I realized why no one goes out to hunt moles.

When the summer rains came we placed buckets where it dripped and put the kids in the room most free of mosquitoes. The days were light and airy or hot and oppressive or both. The nights were always cool, delightful. The colors of the land startled. Lush golds and greens, scarlets, yellows, magentas. Cezanne, Gauguin. Bright days offered up sunsets that exploded in color. With little in the way of competing light, the nights, where there was no cloud cover, were brilliant, shattering, extravagant with stars. So much space. During the day we wandered over the hills and made love and lay nude on the rocks. We played nude volleyball on the weed-filled lawn, fleeing into the barn when a car drove by. A row of eighty-year-old sugar maples lay on the ridge that pointed to the house. We found old sap buckets in the summer kitchen. A Home Comfort wood cooking stove kept us warm on cool days.

One year we stayed up for the summer. We were afraid to turn on the electric, fearing the old wires would burn when forced to carry modern current. We used kerosene lanterns. I wrote poems about a moon butterfly and left them by an open window and one night it rained, blotting the poem, blotting most of it, so that what remained was a haunting fragment of something that in its absence was greater than its presence. We picked blueberries when they appeared and blackcaps and wild raspberries and bought our milk from the farmer down the road, unhomogenized and unpasteurized and we all drank it, spooned out the thick cream for cornflakes and coffee. Friends came up. One couple left screaming in the middle of the night, crazed by bugs. What was the big fuss about bugs? We were purple-hearted from them. Beavers dammed a stream in the back meadow and flooded it. Each morning I went out and spent hours laboriously chopping a hole in their dam and each evening they repaired it and I went out the next day and damaged their repairs. This went on for two weeks, the beavers and I in a great test of wills and stupidity. Finally I quit. (A year later the state used dynamite and that did not work either.) We had a garden and ate fresh lettuce and tomatoes every day and went to a drive-in movie before it was abandoned, and when it got too hot and I was sweaty from destroying beaver dams, we took the kids to a swimming hole in a nearby village, population one hundred and twenty, and after swimming went to a local bar and drank beer and gave the kids sodas, all they wanted, and Slim Jims, and played sand hockey and then drove back to the farm.

I dreamed of building on the property. I needed to know about wood. I wanted to talk to someone about trees.

There was an old farmer down the road. He no longer earned his living as a farmer but in many ways he was still a farmer. He was a short, wizened man with an old-time name. He had a sort of sad happiness about him, a kind of look I had seen on many people up here. Eldon. I never talked to him about trees but he talked to me, to us, about a lot of things. When we first bought the farm we invited him over and since we had no furniture we sat on the floor. He told us about the land, about the kind of men who lived here, all the way back to the civil war. He remembered stories, and hearing them I thought someone should write them down. They should not be forgotten. Of course, they were. The only thing I remember about these stories was how I must not forget them. At the end of the summer we drove back to the city with $50 and no job. It was time to find work and be responsible. It was somewhere in the seventies. Years later the house and the barn needed vast, expensive repairs. We could not afford them. We sold the house and the barn but kept most of the land. The new owners graciously allowed us to come up and use the house, which they were fixing up. And then in the summer of 1992, it suddenly hit me. I had to build. I had to take the timber from our woods. It was an imperative. There was no questioning it.

Money.

YEARS AGO I REALIZED I wasn't much good at making money. I don't know why it took me so long to realize this. Probably the same reason that keeps me from making much money.

There should be no shame here. I know people like this. We eke out a living, and it takes care of the things we need and deprives us of the things we want, until we reach a point where the things we want are more important than the things we need.

I used to think making money was almost dishonorable. A very quirky idea. It was not a concept that had much staying power.

Being out of work, which was happening with increasing frequency, I would often look around the house to see what had to be repaired. Holding a hammer was a source of joy. I thought perhaps that I should become a carpenter, like my grandfather.

I did some trim work, built decks. It did not go well. Money was made, but barely enough to live on.

Decks have a tendency to be built above something else. Most of my time was spent hauling lumber up and hauling waste wood down, or the other way around. Tools had to be brought up, made ready, then carried down again. With decks it was a matter of incessant hammering . . . hundreds, thousands of nails pushed through wood. A nail gun made sense. I would not use one.

One was always making concessions in wood. Every job seemed to bring problems and that caused one to compromise, construct a less than perfect fasten, and that led to another compromise, and so on.

Or the measurement was off, just a bit, but enough to cause further measurements to be off. One carpentered against an existing structure that had settled, leaned, swelled, shrunk, moved, tilted in some unpredictable way, and one had to accommodate the carpentry to that. I was looking for the perfect carpentry job, the job where the wood went together on the site as it had in my mind. Copernican carpentry with Aristotelian angles where the ideal and the real became one. This did not happen. One could be perfect in steel, one had to be perfect in steel, but wood . . . wood was too human. Wood swayed the way the mind swayed; it changed, warped, twisted, cracked, was full of hidden knots and recesses, cavities you couldn't see on the surface the way you couldn't see how the mind bubbled up strange conclusions when put under stress.

Life is a constant struggle between those who never do anything because they want it to be perfect, and they are such perfectionists that they realize the futility of their quest . . . and those who rush ahead in blind fury and do everything, simply everything, and it is not perfect, it is never perfect. It is only the agonized mind that makes a thing close to perfection because the agonized mind holds these two opposing views at the same time. It will never get done. It will always get done. Never. Always.

The wrong way to build a house.

I HAVE NOTHING AGAINST ARCHITECTS. For people who want to build a house with none of the joy of building I suppose they are necessary. But I have never understood why architects should have all the fun designing while you get stuck with the bills.

A house isn't so precious. It should have a roof that doesn't leak, or hardly leaks. It should be reasonably warm. Some windows to let in the sun and air when and where you want them would be nice, and also to keep them out when you don't. The windows should give good views. They should be reasonably large, reasonably efficient. It doesn't make too much difference where the living room, dining room, or kitchen is. They can all be the same room. A few bedrooms, upstairs. A bathroom. Water. Plumbing. Electricity. Maybe a cellar, maybe not. A porch, yes.

The best-looking houses I've seen have been toy houses, the kind you find in children's books, the kind that come in Disney cartoons. They seem very cozy to me. Whatever house I build, this would be my model.

I had three other criteria. First, I simply wanted to build and I wanted to have fun building. Building a house was a good excuse to build. Second, I wasn't too worried about mistakes, except that I didn't want the house to fall over, sink, or rot. Third, I wasn't too worried about money because we didn't have much. I would build it as cheap as I could and then go into debt. I would go in debt to get what I wanted. That way I could look around me and see all the money I owed. And fourth, I wanted to build out of wood. I love wood. Did I say I had three criteria? I had one. I wanted to build a house out of wood. Large pieces of wood. Heavy timbers.

Something else. Where I put the house. This should be a special place, a place that felt right. For me that is in the north where the weather changes and the seasons come by fours. It should be a place that is away from cities and from people who want to get away from cities. You can't be any more precise than that.

Timber dreams.

DREAMING OF WOOD can mean something else, but it can also mean just dreaming of wood. The idea was to make a home out of huge logs pulled from the woods. They would be shaved just enough to find the square. The weave of big timbers would hold this house. It would be like living inside a forest, the air thick with the odor of resin. Great beams, thigh-thick, the wood pinned and slotted together. The slice of the saw would highlight the river of grain that ran through the trees. The rough cut of the saw would show its fuzzed unruly hairs. It would not have the planed finish of a commercial mill, its fussy ink-stamped logo ruining the wood. This was timber. I wanted these big timbers close enough to feel, rough enough to bother my hands.

The meadow rose to a ridge of pine and maple.

SPRING RAINS made it lush and green but just before it was hayed the meadow was a rich yellow. Cut, it was a stubble of green and tan. A creek wandered across it, throwing up a fence of brown grass at the edges. Low bushes dotted the meadow. A slim island of rock sheltered an old apple tree planted years ago. At one corner, near the road, the glacier had carved two smaller ridges and a little valley. An old thorn apple tree clung to one rock, and where the rocks gave out and the funnel of the valley began, we decided to put our home. We planned the layout according to the views. From the kitchen you could see the thorn apple, and then an old oak at the fence line. Turn around and through the dining-room window was the meadow, and beyond that the ridge and then the beginnings of the woods. The meadow was part of a long valley that followed a river. To the north, west, south, you could see the swirls of clouds and the darkening weather as it swept through the valley. This land had been home to many farmers, more than now. During the Civil War thirteen families lived on a stretch of road that now contains just three. There was a foundry at Coopers Falls that made cannon balls.

Hammer. Nail. Wood.

You can still find rusted wagon wheels in the woods where there was a road to the foundry. As a boy, Eldon Wells heard the old men talk about it, and about the strange men who would appear on the road after the war.

Pine, beech, oak, ash, elm, maple, and hemlock.

F A L L . It is quiet in the woods. The bugs are gone. When the weather is dry there is a slow rain of leaves and with the weather wet a slow rain of water. Trees soften the rain, the wind, the weather, the noise. We cut trails to the hemlock we will drag out. Hemlock splits easily, but it is strong wood, good for posts and beams. We look for tall, thick trees, straight trees that contain the twenty-foot 8-by-10 and 8-by-12 timbers we need. These are trees sixty, seventy years old. I never thought I would cut trees. I wanted to grow them.

Chain saws are noisy, hellish. Fat blue clouds of smoke drift up. The first cut terrifies. Wood chips fly, are muddied with oil, and stick to the engine housing.

Eldon had a dairy farm. His milk receipts stayed the same from the 1930s to the 1950s, so he got a job as a night watchman in a factory. His house had no electricity or running water, but his barn did. His barn had its own spring. The factory Eldon worked in has "downsized." How he would have loved that word.

It cracks, buckles, leans.

TREES do not fall where you want them to fall. Sometimes they do not even fall. Chainsawed through, they frequently lean, embraced by other large trees, the tops snagged. Sometimes the saw binds in the wood, tons of timber pinching the blade. The entire tree, fifty, sixty, seventy feet of it, sits on your saw, the weight of the engine bending the blade. Wedges, a sledge hammer to free them. Another chain saw to cut the first one out. Trees get their revenge. Once felled they must be cleaned so they can be snaked out. A stressed branch can kick back with great force when cut. It can put your running chain saw in an uncomfortable place on your body.

Eldon sold his cows but never had electricity put in his house. He had a solid two-story wood house, bright and white, as square and tight as a box. He had the greatest-looking wood stove I've ever seen, an arabesque construction that looked like an Islamic temple but was in fact a temple to wood. He got his water from a pump in the yard. In the winter he got it from the spring that he had piped into the barn. There were three farms side by side. Eldon had one and his father the next two. When his father died he gave them to Donald, Eldon's younger brother. Eldon had a gas refrigerator filled with milk and cold cereal. He had a dozen cats. He took his meals from cans. He never married. When I first met him he was an old man who lived in a harsh world with cold winters. He always had a smile on his face. He told stories he heard as a child about the Civil War and the factories up north and the young men who went off to fight in that war. He never told me much about trees or woods but I liked calling on him and watching him smile. I liked to watch him open the cans of cat food that he set at the foot of his wood stove.

Harlow used to come by and talk to him. Harlow was from a different war, a more modern war. Harlow did not talk to most people. That was just as well.

Look back, go forward, don't stop.

WRAP THE CHAIN around the fallen hemlock, pass it through the tractor bolt and put the hook over a chain link, not through it. Do not start off slowly. Give it plenty of gas and start off with a jerk and once you start moving do not stop, especially uphill, on curves in the trail where you have to snake the log around, even downhill, do not stop, do not tip over, do not wedge the tractor between trees or get hung up on boulders or go flying down a hill so that the log overtakes you and whips the tractor around. Do not. Do not let the log come flying toward you. Do not let the tractor tip over on you. Put the hand brake on when you slip the chain off so the tractor does not slip out of neutral with your hand between the chain and the log.

Harlow is in the woods. He appears early. He does not sleep well in the morning.

Logs tumble, earth shakes.

NOISE, DUST, MUD, LUMBER, SAWDUST, timber, boards, scrap. Pulleys, chains, belts, straps, bolts, pikes, rails, clamps, bars. A 150-horsepower diesel engine. A saw blade the size of a round table (seats eight) rising out of the ground. Steel rails run alongside the blade. A chain runs between them and pulls a steel carriage. The log is clamped onto the carriage bed, held by spikes at the edge away from the saw. One side of the log is over the carriage bed, dangling head first into the blade. The first pass shaves off one side. The log is pulled back and turned, shot through the saw, slab falling to the side, pulled back, turned, run through again. Something long and square emerges, a beam maybe, posts, which may require several more passes to get the sides straight, or it may become flooring, siding, or the wood may be punk and cut for scrap lumber. It is the eye of the operator, the adjustments he makes on the carriage, that gets the most lumber out of the log. It is the death of the log and the birth of lumber, just as the chain saw is the death of the tree and the birth of the log.

Hammer. Nail. Wood.

Harlow comes by way of the river except where the brush covers the riverbank and then he goes through the swamp cedars that grow in the marshy valley that runs along the river.

Dirt, cement.

THE SHOVEL RATTLES like bolts in a can. The engine is slow, has a piston-heavy thud. A mechanical creature, iron arms at both ends, huge landing pods that lift it off the front wheels, one arm with a steel shovel and steel teeth, sliding stainless steel pistons pumped up by tubes of oil, hydraulics, the shovel a curved paw that dips into the ground, clanks, rattles. The engine labors, the shovel comes up with a half ton of earth. Dumps it the way a human hand would, twirling at the wrist of the shovel. Dips down, comes up. Dips down. A square hole. Gravel. Forms for the concrete. Rebars tied together. Pockets for the center joist that will run down the middle. Concrete poured. Bolts placed in the top for the sill. Pressure-treated 2-by-8s. Center beam for the floor from an old barn that blew down in a storm, thirty feet long, eighty years old, gray, the adz marks showing along with the old mortise holes.

Harlow watches us, sitting on a ridge, warm coffee cup in his hands. He doesn't drink the coffee. He brings the coffee out to warm his hands and when the coffee gets cold he throws it away.

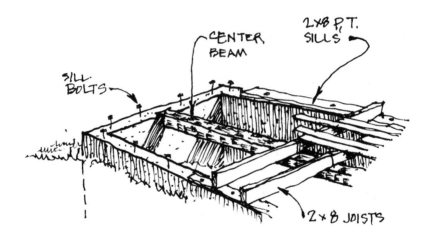

1972 International Harvester.

Paul Simmons drills wells. He works with his father, a UMW member until they closed down the mines by Gouverneur. The steel derrick on the back of the truck is about twenty feet high. A four-cylinder Continental engine lifts the weight up the height of the derrick and then smacks it down on the well-drilling apparatus. The drill head is studded with worn teeth. Once the rig is set up and working, most of the time is spent hanging around, smoking, listening. Paul can tell when something is wrong by the sound—the sound of the Continental engine, the sound of the pipe going through the earth, the rock. Paul likes to buy old pickup trucks for several hundred dollars and keep them running for years. His father wouldn't know what to do if he wasn't working. It takes days to drill. Going through dirt, clay, rock. A river of clay and mud oozes from the hole. Water. But not enough. We doused with brazing rods. All four of us. The water underground yanked the rods down at the same spot. We figured, what the hell. Brazing rods. There must be water there. Fifty, sixty feet. At seventy feet we get seven gallons a minute. Filled three 55-gallon drums. Water. We're standing on it. Paul's father is fiddling with the well-drilling apparatus. He's got a cigarette in his mouth but not many teeth. He's not happy unless he's working.

Build this deck.

THE WOOD COMES BACK FROM THE MILL. Some of it is punky, spongy, with streaks, holes, cracks. Some of it is good. Since the sill is not wide enough to support the footprint of the post, I extend the sill with wood, and reinforce the places under the deck where the posts will rest. Lift the 2½-horsepower Briggs & Stratton engine to the table saw and loop it up. Cut. This was growing wood a week ago. Now, boards. Mose asks me if we should stagger the boards to lock in the joists and I say yes. We do that. I have blocked the joists on top of the center beam. Nail the subfloor on the deck. Mose places the boards with a few nails. I finish the nailing while he goes on to other boards. Whamty bam. Bam, bam. Water oozes out where the nail goes in. Boards gather alongside each other, shoulder to shoulder. So this is what the deck is going to look like. Zam bam. What a good feeling to drive nails into wood. We get down to the last few boards. They're looking worse and we throw away more. We scrounge to come up with the last few boards. Streaks of punk run through some of them, knot holes, cracks. In a former time I would have been fussier, sent them back. But this is wood we cut and going out and buying wood does not seem right. I do not know why. I do not want to cut more wood just for these boards. It's all we can do to get enough timbers for the twenty-foot 8-by-8s and 8-by-12s. This will do. At the end of the day we have the deck covered over, except for a hatch down to the crawl space. The ragged ends of the boards bristle off the sills like stiff hair. I will take a chain saw and trim them straight.

Mose Miller does not work on Friday. He's got too much to do around his farm. He grows corn, potatoes, strawberries, and apples. He makes cider. Friday and Saturday are reserved for that, and of course he will do no work on Sunday. Sunday is church. Monday is frequently half a day because his work spills over into Monday morning and then it takes him an hour to get here by buggy. Tuesday he did not work either. It is a short week. Tuesday is the funeral for the young Amish child who was killed when he fell off the wagon and one of the wheels rolled over him. Mose told me he thought the boy did not suffer much. He was three or four. The entire Amish community was at the funeral. The boy's parents knew that they could ask for anything from the community. They probably would not. They would get along as best they could without bothering people, without even bothering other Amish, and they would keep their anguish and their pain to themselves. It was not something you put out in the open. You kept it in a box, and swallowed the box. If you could. If you could. As there is not much visible anger among the Amish, neither is there much visible pain. Things happen. It is God's will. But the inward pain and suffering, that is something else.

Hemlock.

W E'VE GONE INTO THE WOODS again and made a mess. Can't find the right trees. The big ones are leaning, crooked, curled, or have punk spots on them. We need something longer than twenty feet, much longer, to get our twenty feet and we need it thick, we need to get 8-by-12 out of this tree and we need it straight for twenty feet, with no cracks and as few knots as possible. The chain-saw blade gets stuck and we have to take the blade off and leave it in the tree and try to get it out with wedges and a sledge. We have to take one big crooked tree down to get at one big straight tree and when we do, the straight tree gets hung up on branches. It won't fall. It leans, laughing. We yank at it with the tractor but the big wheels spin in the glacial soil, slipping down to clay. If we don't get these timbers we're in trouble. This is the heart of the house.

Four bents. A bent is a timber H with the top part of the H shaved lower. The posts are the legs of the H, 8-by-10. Twelve feet high. The horizontal part of the H is about nine and a half feet high. The horizontal part is the beam. The two middle

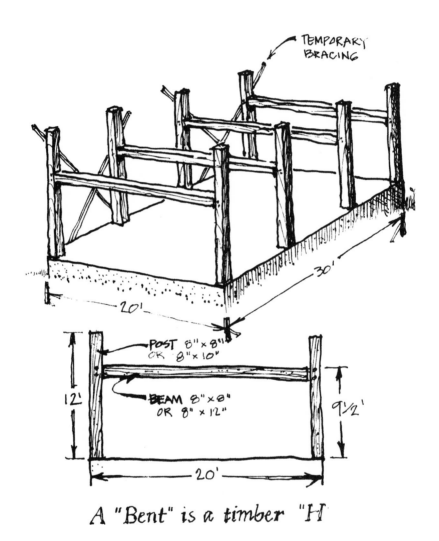

A "Bent" is a timber "H

bents need horizontal beams 8-by-12 because they're going to be carrying more of the roof load than the end bents. The beams for the end bents can be 8-by-8s. Four of the bents spaced at ten-foot intervals constitute the load-carrying structure of the house, which will be twenty by thirty feet. It takes us an hour to get that tree down. At this rate the house will never get built. We do not have a leisurely building schedule; this is not a house built on weekends. Just a month and a half from start to finish. Finish means getting a roof on and getting it covered before winter. It means doing all the bulldozing, the septic system and the drainage, all the earth moving before the ground gets cold and before the spring rains that follow winter turn everything to mud. Not mud really, clay, and you're not turning it to clay but making the clay wet, and wet clay is impossible to work with, impossible to push around. Sometimes it feels like the woods wants you to cut trees down. Something in the woods says, here, take this tree, cut it, and you do and it goes quickly and easily as if it was already cut and had already fallen and all you did was turn a key that set the whole thing going. Sometimes the woods wants you to take a tree out and you chain it to the back of the tractor and start off with a yank and it slides on the earth like a leaf in rain. Sometimes, it doesn't.

This feels like one of those times. The chain keeps slipping down the trunk. Finally we get the tree down but we can't pull it to the trail because a huge maple is in the way. We try rolling the tree, and roll it into a stump. Then we pull it back. The tractor is not powerful enough to yank it around the tree. Too much of the pulled tree is on the wrong side of the pulled-around tree. There's no room for a bigger tractor in these woods, not unless you cut a bigger trail, which means more time cutting trail and less time cutting trees. Trees, of course, are in no hurry. Trees have lots of time. They're stuffed with time. Yanked, twisted, jerked, rolled; we finally work the tree around the offending maple. The bark is heavily chafed where the chain has rubbed. Pulling the tree out with the tractor, I try to imagine what the wood will be like. The grain in the wood is like a river. It curves and flows the way the current flows in water, its eddies and swirls the knots in the wood. And like a river current these are not always apparent on the surface. A knot may be buried in the wood, the branch having broken off years ago and the tree growing around it. There may be cracks buried in the wood, pinholes, or "shelling," where the rings pull away and weaken the wood. Much of this you won't know until you take the tree to the sawmill and cut it for timber. The long, sliced slabs will reveal the current in the grain, will tell you what you can use the wood for, if anything. The sawmill shows you the truth in a tree, shows you that particular truth of the tree. The trees we're pulling out have fifty, sixty years in them; time enough to develop their own truth, their own particular way of being.

When Eldon died his farm was sold to an Amish family, the Zooks, and the first thing they did was take the electric out of the barn. A house that had never seen kids was packed with them. Beds were brought in. Cupboards, tables, straight-back chairs. Harlow missed Eldon. I did too. When Eldon went a chain was broken, as if the Civil War had finally ended. The Zooks built a sawmill and a school and planted corn where Eldon had never thought about planting anything.

Iron and wood.

STEEL AND LUMBER, IRON AND WOOD. There is no lumber without steel and there is no steel without iron and no iron without the ore and the earth where it comes from, and the trees come from that same earth so that the blade that cuts into the tree, that sophisticated high-technology blade, that alloy blade with a precise carbon content so that it may be tough and yet remain sharp and hard, not too hard to be brittle and break and not too soft so it loses its edge, that steel, that wood, have met before in the earth. They are not strange to each other.

If no one was around I would always apologize to the tree for cutting it. I hope only the tree hears me. The tree could hear and not care. What good do your apologies do? You cut me. No, no, you will rise again, I promise, in a building, and you will have a magnificent view, you will look over a beautiful meadow and see the weather for miles off and inside you, underneath you, will be humans and warmth and laughter and tears, too. Well, this is all silly, certainly is. Apologizing to trees is not something I want to go public with. But I like being around wood, I do, and I hope that in some way, which I

Hammer. Nail. Wood.

do not understand, the tree understands. This is something I keep to myself.

Harlow doesn't do much these days, not after his farm was sold. He was not a very good farmer. No one in his family was, but it was his unluck to be at the end of the line when years of bad farming finally caught up. It is the medicine that keeps him going, that and the visits to Emile and Skyler.

Sex and wood.

I HAVE BEEN OBSESSED for weeks now with this house, this home, the building of it. Thinking of nothing else, or very little else. Even sex flits by less than it did. The heart of the house is the bents, and the heart of the bents is the places where the posts and beam join. This is a marriage, a sexual union in wood. The post is female. It has a tunnel precisely etched in wood to receive the tongue or tenon of the beam. This tunnel is called a mortise. The mortise is three inches wide, placed in the center of the post about nine and a half feet high, and it goes all the way through the post. It is eight or twelve inches deep, depending on the beam, and sits in a shoulder or groove one inch deep that runs the height of the mortise. This shoulder provides additional support for the heavy beam, and also guards against shear, or a tendency for the beam to twist. The tenon or tongue of the beam is three inches by nine inches. The post is ten inches in depth, the extra inch accounting for the shoulder. The tenon goes all the way through the post and is flush with the far side of the mortise. Both mortise and tenon must be tight and precise. One-quarter-inch error will throw the whole bent out of square over the course of twenty feet. If the fit is too tight the wood will split. If it is too loose the joint will wobble and slide apart. You may have a half-ton of wood falling from nine feet. After the mortise and tenon are joined together and the square of the timbers checked, holes are drilled for the insertion of one-inch-diameter hardwood pins, which run through mortise and tenon, locking them together. Knee braces, a triangulation with wood, may be added for further rigidity. Then the bent is raised and locked to the deck. If it is a conventional deck the bent can be spiked to the deck. If the sill is a timber, however, and you would like to do more work, and add a complication, you can mortise and tenon the post of the bent to the timber sill. This provides great rigidity but demands extreme precision. You do not want to be more than one-quarter, preferably one-eighth, of an inch off. Drop a plumb bob from the middle of the beam to check your perpendicular, or, if you are more adventurous, have someone stand back and eyeball the bent. You want it straight.

Harlow bought a Plymouth Slant Six from Skyler, but he didn't want to buy it, he said it didn't sound right, a Slant Six sounded skewed, but Skyler told him that a Slant Six was the straightest engine around and that it would outlast his junk-yard, and he kept on talking until finally just to shut him up Harlow bought that Plymouth and found out that it had indeed a mighty fine engine. It was too good an engine. The Japanese told Chrysler to stop making it because it lasted too long, they could never build anything that lasted that long. The tires were another story. "I don't trust the tires," Skyler told Harlow. "They are radial tires and they have steel in them, steel wires, and they run through the rubber and I do not know if rubber can stand that. I have a set of American tires I can sell you, used American tires that have fabric running through them and I would recommend them." But Harlow had made up his mind that he would only listen to Skyler once and he declined the offer to trade the radial tires for a set of American tires. Several weeks later one tire had a blowout, and it shook the car and threw Harlow out of the car and he skidded down the highway on his head.

Tools you need and some you might not.

ONE OF THE NICE THINGS about building is that you get to buy tools you don't have. Then you get to use them. Watch how someone uses a tool. You can tell a lot about that person. What you find out may not be particularly pleasant. You can also find out about yourself. As you use the tool, the tool uses you. You'll find out what you are like by watching yourself. It always works both ways. If you are building in an area like the one we built on, with no electricity, you must plan your tool library accordingly. The Amish overcome the need for power tools by bringing their power with them. In addition to the usual set of hand tools they frequently bring along a 2½-horsepower Briggs & Stratton stationary gasoline engine. This little dynamo is used to power table saws, beam-boring drills, and cement mixers, among other tools, and is simply bolted where needed. In addition, I have found a chain saw indispensable. Used with extreme care and great caution, it will save you much time and effort. But hand tools, the old-fashioned muscle-using type, are the heart and soul of any timber-framing operation. You will want a good hand rip saw and a good crosscut saw. Buy the best. Keep the blades sharp.

When you make your cut, keep your kerf square so the saw doesn't bind on you. A saw that binds is letting you know that the cut you are making will not be square, nor will it be straight if you are cutting on an angle. Despite my predilection for American tools, I use a Japanese timber-framing saw, both for its accuracy and for the delightful way it cuts. Japanese saws cut on the pull. This allows them to have a thinner blade and the result is a narrower, finer, more precise saw cut.

The cut.

THE FIRST CUT YOU MAKE IS CRUCIAL. After the sawmill gives you timbers, this is the cut that squares the timbers. Use a framing square, an L-shaped piece of steel, 16 inches by 24 inches. You want to make the end of each timber nice and even, as square and as perpendicular to its length as possible so it will sit absolutely flat on the deck. For purposes of perfection, we will ignore imperfections, dips and rises that will probably occur in the deck, even over a short distance. You will want to find the side of the timber that looks the straightest. Eyeball it down its length. Lay the long axis of the framing square along the length of the timber and mark a perpendicular with a sharp carpenter's pencil (those stubby octagonal pencils that fit so easily in your hand) on one side. The idea now is to run that first perpendicular continually around the timber as one line. Using the same reference edge draw a perpendicular with the framing square that extends the line you have just drawn to the other plane. Now roll the timber over and extend that line using the edge of the timber that is directly opposite on the square of the edge you have used for your first reference edge. Extend these lines in both directions. The continuous lines should meet exactly and should also be in square. If not, start over. Use another edge. Check how you lined up your square. This pencil-marked square that you are drawing around the timber will be your saw guideline for squaring off the end of your timber. Take the time here to get it right and you will get a perfect, near perfect, square. The block of wood that comes off the timber will reveal a nice flat surface. It will be a delight to run your hand over that surface, to feel the coolness of the wood, and to feel its flatness. After you have made such a flat cut you will feel very good for at least three minutes. The secret to squaring your timber is to first have your penciled square scribed around the timber so that it is perpendicular to the edges, or perpendicular to the best edge, and also to make sure that it meets evenly at all four corners, that it is a continuous straight line drawn completely around the lumber. Second, make sure you get a proper kerf. The kerf is the channel in the wood the saw rides in, the first depth or groove you put in the wood. If your kerf is straight it guides your saw straight and you can feel it slicing perfectly square through the wood. To get a proper kerf you must keep the saw on your laboriously drawn pencil lines and rock the saw back and forth so you build up the groove on both sides of the timber. The first kerfs on the front and back of the timber will then help you guide the saw so that your downward cut is straight and even. Keep rocking the saw back and forth, directly on your pencil lines. Take great pains to establish the right kerf at the beginning of the cut and that way you will get a nice perpendicular cut. Remember, the timber you are going through is 8-by-8 or 8-by-12. That's a long way to go, and if you're off a little bit in the beginning by the time you reach the end you will be way off. After the end piece comes off, check it once again with the framing square on at least two sides of the timber. If it still

Hammer. Nail. Wood.

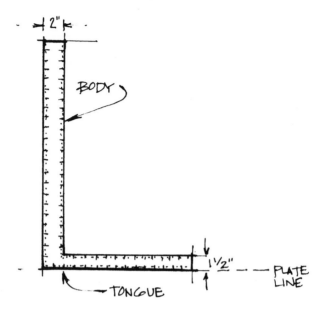

2"

BODY

1½"

PLATE
LINE

TONGUE

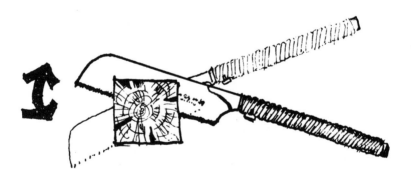

needs a little bit of shaving to make it square take a block plane, a small plane that fits in the palm of your hand, and very carefully shave off what's needed to make it square. Keep checking with the framing square until that framing square snugs up evenly to the end of the timber. Then measure out the exact length you need for the timber and repeat the process for the other end. Making the mortise and tenon with the slick and the chisel will be talked about separately. You will want to make sure these cuts are squared and perpendicular, so you will use a combination square, a small steel measuring ruler with a groove that runs down the center and holds a sliding gizmo that gives you a perpendicular off the ruler. This way you can check both at the beginning and the end of the mortise, and the tenon, and make sure your cuts are square. By sliding this perpendicular piece up and down the ruler, you can check the perpendicular on cuts that are as little as one inch or as deep as twelve. You'll also get a good measurement at the same time.

90° & 45° MOST FREQUENTLY USED LAYOUTS IN TIMBER FRAMING

Drill and drive.

IN ORDER TO LOCK THE MORTISE AND TENON together you will drill a hole and drive wood pins in through both joints. These wood pins must be hardwood. Birch is the most common doweling in hardware stores. Those are hardwood and they will work fine, but if you are very particular you might want to use oak, walnut, cherry, or maple dowels. They should be one inch in diameter. This means that you will need a drill bit one inch in diameter, and at least fifteen inches long, and a good brace to hold the drill bit if you intend to drill the hole by hand, plus strength and patience. After you've drilled the holes for the pins (once the mortise and tenon are already joined and squared), you need a mallet to knock the pins in. Do not use a steel hammer; you don't want to crack the wood pins. The mallets can be wood or neoprene.

What else? Perhaps a corner chisel for the corners in the mortise. A good set of sharpening stones for your chisels and slick. Use several sharpening stones, ending up with the smallest grained stone you can buy. Use oil or water on the stone, depending on your style of stone, to get the straightest

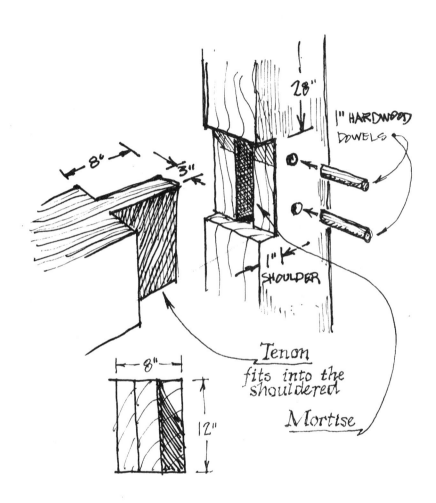

28"

1" HARDWOOD DOWELS

8"

3"

1" SHOULDER

Tenon
fits into the
shouldered
Mortise

8"

12"

edge. Then use a strop with a strop paste of aluminum oxide to get the final edge. You should be able to shave with your chisel's edge.

Anything else? A good strong set of hemp ropes or movers' slings to hold the bents when you raise them. And a come-along if you have no backhoe, derrick, or about twelve or fifteen pairs of hands to help you raise the bents. A come-along has two steel hooks on cables that come out of a steel box, with a ratchet handle at the top. Properly attached, you can raise several tons by hand with a come-along. Get a good twenty-ounce hammer, a tape measure, and a scribe. They'll all come in handy.

They said he walked on his head. They said he danced on his head. They said the sight of Harlow going down the road on his head was one of the most mysterious sights they had ever seen. And Harlow, what did he think about that? Was he prepared for the dreams that came to him when he ambled down the road? Did he think about everything he had done when he saw, not his life, but the road flashing before him? I believe that God held His hand under Harlow's head as he danced down the road. I think that God wanted to tell him something, wanted to give Harlow more time so he could tell him something. Harlow did not think so, but when it comes to what God thinks it makes no difference what we think, does it?

Old tools, worn tools, used tools.

THERE ARE SEVERAL WONDERFUL PLACES up north, in Maine, Vermont, New Hampshire, and New York state, that sell old tools, used tools, worn tools. They are sold in ancient buildings, dark and wooden with uninsulated wooden walls and windows that rattle in well-weathered frames. If there is anything close to nirvana it is wandering into one of these places on a Saturday afternoon. Make that a Saturday morning. You don't want to rush this, you want to go easy into this gray dawn. These are not antique stores, and people whose idea of iron is something cast and frilly and painted black would be advised to stay away. The people that run the places I am thinking about are not particularly polite and obsequious the way antique dealers are. Much of the stuff they sell is junk, the kind of stuff that looks so bad you'd be ashamed to throw it away near your house. Crap when it was new, and more so now. But much of the other stuff, tools, old iron tools, frequently wrought iron, is delightful. So delightful it makes me squirm. Don't let anyone try to sell you something new and tell you it is wrought iron, because it isn't.

Hammer. Nail. Wood.

I am thinking of one used tool store in Maine that frequently has some old tool chests on the front porch, an anvil that isn't rusted to death, and as you go in, about twenty old saws hanging from a shelf. The sight of those saws will suck the wind right out of you. To see the shimmer and sheen in a row of old saw blades and their wonderfully scrolled oak handles with the brass rivets that fix them forever to the blade, oh my! And blacksmith's tongs! Oh, please! A long row of them, their legs straddling a horizontal wood pole as if they were all about to climb over, and if that weren't enough, several old oak dynamite cases, the sticks they contained long ago exploded, holding dozens of standing tongs jammed together like lean, angry dogs. Pick up a pair of tongs and heft them in your hands. If they are old enough they are probably wrought iron. You can tell by the grain in the iron, like the grain in wood. Those tongs feel good in your hands! Open and close, feel the weight, the balance. Look at the lips, probably scarred and ragged. You want to be a blacksmith just to hold these tongs and then you want to buy dozens of tongs, heavy black wonderful iron, tongs for every occasion, for holding every possible shape that metal may come in, and you will also need anvils and hammers and swage blocks and a good blacksmith's vise and of course a forge and blower, and this wonderful five-story shop in this small town in Maine has all this and much more, yes, much more. Taps and dies, sheetmetal molds—heavy iron shapes that look like the parts to a Buck Rogers rocket—tons of hammers, sledge hammers, dozens of tool chests, nail pullers, draw bars that fit on tractors, logging chains, logging pikes and logging peaveys, beautiful old power drills with stainless steel casings from companies that only knew how to make a good power drill, not a cheap one, and so went bankrupt, hundreds of braces to hold drill bits and thousands of drill bits in oily metal tin trays sticking out of a stew of ant scat and crusts of spider webs on the bottom, beam borers that rest on a beam and hand crank a drill bit through eight inches of beam, old chain saws that have cut through enough wood to build small cities, their chains now worn and loose on the bar but still glistening through decades of dirt and oil, hundreds of levels, some canoe shaped, twelve inches long, gray with age, the vials broken and yellowed, dust dry, and some eight and ten feet long with dozens of vials at various intervals along the way (I bought one that was a foot long, thumb smooth oak, and one of the vials even worked, an oblong brass plate tacked into the center, a four-inch ridge running along the side so you could have something to play your finger upon), huge hooks, pulleys, printing presses, iron bars, barrels of rusting nails welded into a stunning clump of iron oxide, fishing poles from the forties and tackle boxes full of scales and fish oil and not just fish blood but worm blood and human blood, type fonts, type trays, cast iron cooking and heating stoves, medals from the honorable wars and weapons from same, box and open-end wrenches from the tiny to the tremendous (I bought an adjustable wrench, not the silly piece of Taiwan metal you get today, but a real adjustable wrench with square jaws, a wooden handle framed in iron, a knurled thumb screw and the screw that did the adjusting not knife sharp and breakable but wide and flat, a proper screw that can take a lot of pressure, and the large jaw that it adjusted made from iron, the entire wrench shiny from use, not design, the metal gray and pitted, dimpled, wavy, full of nicks and scratches, and stamped on the top: COES WRENCH CO, WORCESTER, MASS, USA, heavy when you pick it up, and one of the finest mechanical motions you can ever make in your life is turning the knurled knob and watching the moveable jaw slide up), wrenches from those as long as your finger to those as long as your leg, acres of block planes, the iron and steel blades angled in the opening of old hard-wood—oak, cherry, walnut—that is dark and oiled and gleaming with age (I bought a dado plane that puts a curved groove near the edge of a piece of wood, a thin plane that fits comfortably within your hand and has a long steel blade with a curved tip on the end), watches, frying pans, cameras, 78-rpm records, there are not enough commas in the universe to separate all the tools this store in Maine has. And in northern New York state there is an old man who sells, in addition to many of the above tools, old stationary engines, dinosaurs of internal combustion with flywheels the size of frying pans. These ancient engines do not so much run as wheeze their way through four cycles, but the sound they make is the most human sound you will ever hear an internal combustion engine make. There are people today who think that the noise of an old stationary engine is the most magnificent sound in the world. They put it right up there with the sound of the sea on a pebble beach, or rain in an oak forest.

You must find these places for yourself. You must buy old tools not just for their looks, oh no, though you will do that. You must buy them because the spirit of being used well is in them and they will guide your hand in the right way, they will help you, they will select the straight edge, help you find the level and the square, the perpendicular cut, the absolutely flat smash of hammer on nail head. Old tools are full of wise spirit, especially really old tools, and this is because those tools that do not have this wisdom break quickly, never last. These old tools are not machine-made, that is, the machine that made them had a human being behind it, and frequently that human being stamped his name on the tool. To use these tools is to enjoy the counsel of a sage and patient mentor, a cabinetmaker, a master craftsman. For the bargain hunters among you, do not think the owners of these stores will sell these tools cheap. Many of these shops I've been in, loved, bought old tools from, had numerous items that were overpriced. I never saw a real bargain in these stores. But then I wasn't looking for something cheap. I was looking for something worthwhile.

Harlow had a job turning brake drums in Potsdam. Mostly he worked on Brockways and Peterbilts, Whites and Macks, logging trucks. The drivers had let the brakes go too long and the brake shoes had worn down to the rivets and the rivets scraped against the drum making a racket and that's how the drivers knew that they needed their brakes relined. They also had to have the drums turned because the rivets scored grooves in the drums and while you didn't absolutely positively need to turn the drums when you put in a new set of brake shoes, if you didn't it would reduce the area of braking surface by the width of the scored rivet on the drum. You could take a chance with that. Logging trucks took a chance with a lot of things and some of them were willing to take a chance with that, but for others, the idea of coming down an Adirondack hill with twenty or thirty tons of logs behind you and needing to hit the brakes somewhere along the descent made them pause. Maybe, maybe it was a good idea to have the drums turned. Maybe they would need that extra bit of brake. Harlow turned the drums on a lathe. One day he turned a drum down so much it disappeared. He was willing to go on working the drum, grind it down more, but the absence of the drum prevented him.

He worked in a welding shop, stick welding, repairing the broken links on logging chains that had snapped. Then he unloaded grain sacks at the Agway in Heuvelton. There was a propane station where you dropped off empty and picked up full. He helped out when they needed. There were signs up that said no smoking. NO SMOKING. They meant it. Everyone smoked, all the time, everywhere, but not around propane. Even so, a small propane tank blew up and Harlow was lifted clean off his feet, as if a giant hand had finger-flicked him. He was a long time in the air and had a lot of time to think while he was in the air. It made Harlow think about the wonder of being here. It was a gift, being here.

Mortise and tenon. The slick.

SOMEONE ONCE TOLD ME that the hemlock in Maine was better than the hemlock in New York. He said it was straighter, stronger, the grain tighter. He was from Maine. He knew I was going to build my house in New York, above the Adirondacks, just twenty miles below the St. Lawrence River. He settled back when he said it, and got a Maine look on his face. Well, I thought. Well.

The tenon is the easier cut. It is roughed out with a saw and the final dimensions are cut with a slick. A slick is a long chisel that is worked by hand, without mallet or hammer. It is the premier tool in timber building. Many craftsmen carry them in their own case. The most expensive are made in Japan. So are the cheapest. They are hollow ground, and when properly sharpened will cut a rested finger. Used correctly they impart a smooth, almost liquid surface to the wood, shaving off paper-thin strips until the exact dimension is reached. You work the slick with both hands, standing over the wood to use the weight of your body. You ease the slick across the grain or along the grain. The wood will tell you which direction it likes. The slick is not to be used to pry wood off. The blade might chip at the end. Japanese chisels and slicks are made from harder steel than British or American. They hold an edge better but can be brittle in the hands of a clumsy user. British or Japanese chisels can be used for timber framing. American chisels are tougher but softer, and do not hold an edge as well. They are less likely to be damaged by a clumsy user but lack the precision needed for framing.

Harlow was in a war that most of us have forgotten about. In between the Second World War and the Vietnam War, it was in-between in other ways. We won the Second World War and we lost the Vietnam War, but we had no idea if we won or lost the Korean War. When Harlow came back he had no idea either but it was not particularly important to him. He came back. That was important to him. He thought he would work on the farm but the farm was like the Korean War, and then it became more like the Vietnam War. He bought himself a Kawasaki motorcycle and did some heavy drinking and then, in one of those strange mysteries of life, stopped heavy drinking and turned it into light drinking. No one held that against him. There wasn't much else to do in the evening up north. The thought was that he had found something else to do and they were curious. Many people either drank in bars or drank at home. If they did neither of these they spent a lot of time in church. Harlow did none of these. He was as puzzled as everyone else about it.

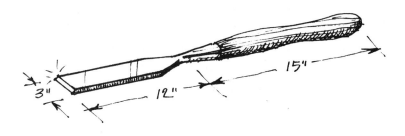

Mortise and tenon. The chisel.

Mortise is the woman part of wood. I could say the female part of wood, but that doesn't aptly characterize the mortise. It is harder to make than the tenon, which is worked from the outside. The mortise is worked from the inside. It constantly expands, and then it stops at precisely the right moment. Ideally, it is the exact mold of the tenon, which must slide in with just the proper degree of tightness and perpendicularity. Watching the two being fitted together, the one slowly pounded into the other, can cause no small feeling of excitement. With the tenon fitted flush to the outer edge of the post, and the entire cross-section of the beam precisely engulfed by the post so that the shoulder is tight and one can see the joint and yet not slip a piece of paper in between, that experience is one of utmost exhilaration. It rarely happens. It is the ideal. Oh, the exhilaration happens when the two pieces of wood come together. The union is thrilling. But remember, not only does the joint have to fit perfectly, with fourteen edges matching exactly, but the post and beam must be perpendicular, and I mean perpendicular not for a few feet, but for twenty feet, and both post and beam must lie in the same plane, with all faces flush, and the gap, there simply is no gap, there is the joint that we can't even slip a piece of paper into. Yet wood is organic, never perfect. Perfect is not organic. Perfect is not natural. The wood will bend and twist, the grain will distort slightly, knots will throw it off, and if wood looks perfect when it's green, wait until it dries. No, wood is not perfect. Ideas are perfect. Steel is closer to perfect. A joint in wood is a novel, a short story. In the hands of an artist it may come close, especially if the artist has the best wood, the right tools. But failure hovers over it all. *Moby Dick, The Sound and the Fury, Fear and Trembling* are all failures, but what failures. To have a failure like that!

The cutting edge of a chisel is also a failure of sorts. To be properly hard and capable of keeping a sharp edge the carbon content of the steel must be increased. But then the edge becomes brittle. Reduce the carbon content, soften the steel, and the edge becomes tougher, harder to chip, but also loses its edge, which becomes rounder. The best chisels for timber framing are British and Japanese. They are large, wide chisels and feel good in the hand. They are also expensive compared to plastic-handled, factory drop-forged chisels. I use a British chisel made by Robert Sorby, a wonderful instrument. Japanese chisels take two billets of steel and join them. The first has a soft iron or steel body for toughness. This is joined to the second, a steel cutting-edge with a higher carbon content that can be hardened to keep its edge. This blade is inserted into a wood socket with a steel tang to hold it on and a steel hoop at the end of the handle so the wood will not spread when hit. A chisel that is used for wood is never hit with a steel hammer but with a wooden mallet or, more recently, a neoprene mallet. A chisel cut in wood is not meant to be made explosively or instantaneously. That is the kind of hit one would get with

Mortise and tenon. The chisel.

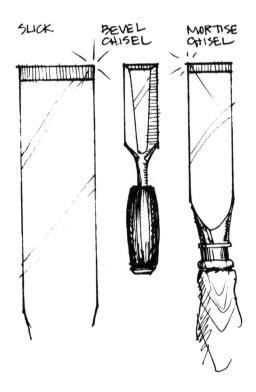

SLICK   BEVEL CHISEL   MORTISE CHISEL

a steel hammer. But it should be *almost* instantaneous. The "spring" in the wood or neoprene unleashes a sudden drive that flows through the tool without marring the wood. The point here is not to leave a mark in the wood but to caress off the excess fibers, to "convince" the wood to give up layers of itself in a way that keeps as much of the smoothness and natural sheen of the wood as possible. This is the fit a cabinet-maker wants for a drawer to slide, the joint a timber framer wants when the tenon plunges into the mortise.

Skyler could sell you a car that wouldn't run and have you swearing that it would run, that all it needed was new ignition wires, or clean plugs, or a capacitor. Even after you bought the car and tried to fix it up, did fix it up—if it still wouldn't run you felt ashamed of yourself for not getting it running. You would not bring that car back to Skyler and tell him the damn thing wouldn't run. No. You would try harder to get that car to run. And if you saw Skyler, if he drove by your place and asked you how your car was, you'd feel ashamed. "How's it running?" Skyler would ask, in that pleasant sort of raspy voice he had. And you'd be ashamed to tell him that it wasn't running. You'd feel that you had let him down, that you had ruined what had been a perfectly good car, a fine car, that only needed a small adjustment, something minor, a little tinkering. Now you had gone and botched it, ruined the car forever. You hated to admit that to Skyler. He had in good faith sold you a perfectly fine automobile, and you had taken it and just ruined it. "How's it running?" Skyler would ask again.

Deck full of timber.

EMILY THEIBAULT was married to Emile Theibault. E & E they called them. Emile also ran a junkyard, began doing so when he was running the town dump and started to bring stuff home and leave it in the front yard of his farm until he could decide what to do with it. One day when he was sitting in the kitchen, which was the only really warm room in his house, he knew what to do with it. He would leave it in the front yard. Emily, or Em, drove the town school bus. She said this was a fine job. One spring-thawed day with the fields full of gray mud and tan stubble she turned the corner and looked up in the rear view mirror. The devil was following her. She took her hands off the wheel and turned around to the children and said, "It's in the hands of God now." It was. It was.

The deck now is filled with big timbers and we have to put them together, fit them together, marry them in that mystical union called a joint and then raise them, somehow raise them so they stand, solid and straight, and attach them. *We* is Mose, his helper Andy, and myself. But it is I who have hired Mose and Andy, it is I who is paying them by the hour, so it is I who feels the burden of this project, this house, these timbers. I've been to timber-framing school in Maine for a week, and now I'm an expert in mortise and tenon and getting joints to fit snug, proper. Mose announces this, with a not-so-hidden chuckle, to Andy. "He's going to show us how to do it," Mose says. Of course Mose has built Amish barns before so this kind of joinery is not new to him. It is to me though. And how will the three of us pull this off? I've got to get these up in a few more days. Finished, enclosed, roofed, in two and a half weeks. I'm going away and won't be back until spring. Look at those huge timbers! And I need eight mortise and tenon joints. Eight, damn it! Holes have to be drilled to speed up the mortise joints. A mud-gray sky slides across. Just a few moments ago it was blue and warm. Now rain. A huge black plastic cover is dragged over most of the deck. The three of us are whittling, chipping, cutting in the rain. The rain stops but the sky is swirls of gray. The air is choppy and fresh. The water on the plastic looks like pools of paint, liquid blobs of black mercury that roll when the plastic is disturbed. I've marked and scribed the places on the posts and beams where the mortises and tenons go. We've unhooked the 2½-horse Briggs & Stratton from the table saw and brought it over to a beam-boring drill. If we can find the right pulley it can be attached and held onto the beam so the drill doesn't override the mortise marks. Then the mortise can be roughed out with the chisel and finished with the slick. The mortise is three inches wide and should be in the middle of the post. It should start on one side in the middle, and exit eight inches later on the other side in the middle. This mortise should be a perfectly square tunnel, its sides parallel to the sides of the post and running perpendicular to the length of the post. The channel for the shoulder should be one inch deep, square and smooth. The tenon can

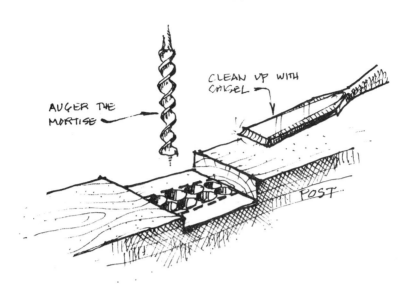

AUGER THE MORTISE

CLEAN UP WITH CHISEL

POST

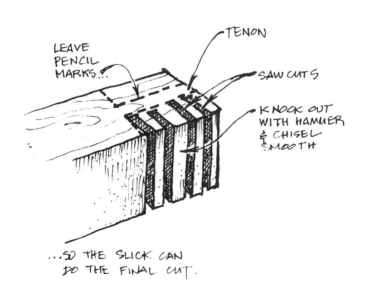

LEAVE PENCIL MARKS...

TENON

SAW CUTS

KNOCK OUT WITH HAMMER & CHISEL SMOOTH

...SO THE SLICK CAN DO THE FINAL CUT.

be roughed out with the saw, with slice cuts an inch wide across the beam almost to the depth of the tenon and running back almost to the shoulder. The slice cuts are then easy to knock out with a hammer. The finish work is done with the slick. There will be hours, days, using the saw, chisel, slick. It will be felt in the fingers, forearms, shoulders. The chisel is used to straighten out the curved edges left by the drill. A small square is lowered into the mortise to check the walls of the mortise. They should be flat, straight, and tilt neither away or toward any of the sides. Using the flat end of the chisel *away* from the flat side of the mortise gives you more control over the angle of the chisel. It may seem easier to use the flat side of the chisel against the flat side of the mortise, but then there is a tendency for the chisel to dig in and cause the mortise to widen as it descends.

Paul bought his six-cylinder Continental engine that runs the well-drilling rig, which sits on the back of his 1972 International Harvester truck, from Emile. He didn't pay much for it. Emile wasn't sure if it would run and he was willing to take it back if Paul couldn't get it running but there wasn't much Paul couldn't get running, just about any engine, especially if his dad could help him. The Continental ran fine. It had only been idle twenty-five years or so. Emile wanted to sell him a newer International Harvester, a 1975, but Paul didn't see much of a reason for that since he figured he had twenty or thirty more years on his 1972 and by that time he'd be worn out himself, like those ball-studded drill bits he used to grind away through dirt and rock in search of water, sniffing for water, lapping it up. His dad would be gone too by then, and he was just getting used to the '72, no need to switch a newer one on him.

Em, she wasn't hurt in the crash. Not a scratch. Wasn't much of a crash anyway. The kids were disappointed, though you could hardly tell with all their laughing and howling. They thought they ought to miss at least one day of school.

Now, let's not kid ourselves. The people who run junkyards, they come from a different place. You don't think Emile and Skyler got where they are by being dummies, by playing hard to get? Skyler used to parachute off buildings tall enough for his chute to open. But that gave him no satisfaction. Satisfaction was in machinery. He sold airplanes and printing presses, the German presses that were as big as houses and could print the Bulldog edition for a medium-sized city in twenty minutes. The Second World War brought an end to that. He made a fortune in scrap metal during the war. That's what they said. He never said. No one held it against him. No one held anything against Skyler. There was something large about Skyler, even though he was a small man. You felt good around him. People said he was charmed, that having all that air blown in his face from falling off tall buildings, or buildings tall enough to open a parachute, had done something to him, had allowed him to breathe in more *being*. He was not a particularly handsome man, but he knew how to smile. He was able to calm Harlow when many were not, when it was important to calm Harlow.

Getting the horse back.

MOSE HAS A NEW HORSE, a beautiful black gelding. Young. Frisky. Horse spooks when people are around it. Doesn't like to be hitched to the buggy, doesn't like other male horses much, doesn't like cars, barely tolerates Mose. But a puller! Wants always to be moving, stepping, running. If Mose can train him this will be one fine horse, a good buggy horse. You can make good time with this horse. Yes, you can make some fine time with this horse. This morning he's got him tied to a thirty-foot barn beam in the meadow and there's a bucket of oats to keep him amused. One mortise and tenon are ready. We use wooden dowels and roll them together. We lift an end up and put it on wooden blocks that we've cut off to square the ends of the timber. We push them in by hand as far as they will go, which is not very far, and then use a sledge to unite them. This is tricky. You want to be forced to pound hard enough to get a nice square, tight fit, but you don't want to pound so hard you split the wood or end up mushrooming it. We pound it on the post side. Andy holds a block against the post so it won't be pitted with hammer marks while Mose and I take turns pounding. Thunk! Quarter-inch. Thunk! The post is lined up alongside the edge of the deck. You don't want to knock the post off the edge of the deck. Not good. Nor do you want to knock the post to the middle. With each thunk the beam should slide in the mortise eagerly but not too eagerly, accepting the tenon. Keep checking with the framing square. When the resistance is too great you must back out and clean up mortise and tenon to ease the beam's entrance. Knock it in, take it out, scrape out the offending wood, knock it in again, in and out, in and out, until with the final knock you've sent the beam home, flush with the outer edge of the post, nestled snug and tight in the shoulder. You take out the framing square and check the perpendicularity. It should be ninety degrees. Exactly. That's what the book says. That's what the class says. That's what all the experts say who aren't there with you hammering the beam in. Uh huh. Of course it doesn't fit exactly. One side fits tighter than the other. It's not perfectly square. How the hell are you going to get it square now? It's too late, isn't it? And the wood. With this beam, to get an 8-by-12, twenty feet of it, we had to accept a little rounding at the corners near the end, the bark still showing, so it can't fit perfectly in the shoulder, it doesn't quite reach edge to edge on the bottom groove, or the top one either for that matter, it won't be perfect, or even that close to it. Andy and Mose hold one end of the post. I go to the other end of the beam and give it a push, a tap, to get it more perpendicular, and oh shit! I see it bend at the joint! It's scary when big timbers bend. You think, uh oh, I've done it, ruined not just several days work on the joints but two big pieces of timber as well and we don't have extra timbers, not many anyway, can't afford to have them breaking. But relax. I'm the expert. I'm spozed to come up with the solutions. I look up to see if anyone else spotted this momentary bend. No one did. So there. I was the only one who saw it happen. So it hardly happened.

Hammer. Nail. Wood.

It only one-third happened. If it's broken, and I'm not saying its broken, not saying its split, it would only be one-third split at most. I go down the length of the beam to look. Looks fine to me. Quite fine. Beautiful. Like the day. Where the hell is the horse? Mose doesn't seem worried. We work on the other joint and it seems to go easier until we get near the end and then it is harder, much harder, and we go in and out, in and out, pounding and scraping, and I begin to worry that we are scraping too much and the joint will wobble even though we can't yet pound it in and I don't want to pound too hard and end up with a split post, which would ruin, I believe, three pieces of timber and not just two because now we would have to pound the first post out again and everything is so, is so ... so something. What kind of day is this? It is such a beautiful day it aches. I always thought that on a beautiful day the work went well, supremely well, that on a day like this one would get caught up in the Zen of wood (what a horrible conceit! what a dangerous word! what a misleading idea!) and that the whole enterprise would just glide by. That is it. The world, the wood, the joints, the mortises and the tenons and the cuts with chisel and slick, they would all glide. It would be almost too beautiful to behold, to be a part of, to experience. Humans were not meant to experience such joy. The sky dazzles. It is a hurting blue. Can you imagine that the work is not perfect? The wood not perfect? Everything Mose and Andy and I do not perfect? Not I. And yet, there it is. We are pounding, sweating, and all my visions and ideals of the perfect joint, OK, I'd settle for the not-so-perfect joint, the less-than-perfect joint, even the less-than-that perfect joint. I'd settle for that. I want to convince myself that what I am doing is so ecstatically right, so exquisitely beautiful, so marvelously exact that I hardly have to brag about it, at least not much. I will have an awakening in this wood. I am not just building a house, putting together timber, I am having satori, I am having samadhi, I am being awakened! I am changed! I am becoming perfect by realizing how perfectly imperfect I am! This is it! This is the essence of *itness*! Shit! The damn thing still isn't going in right. We pound and pound, in and out, cut away with the slick, and finally: The first bent. OK. There it is. I wanted to feel smug when I finished it, satisfied, changed, glorified. It's finished. At least I feel. I look up at Mose. He looks up at the horse, way out in the field, a black toy against the green, munching, looking up when we notice him, munching. Blue sky, white clouds, green meadow, black horse. The horse should not be out in the fields. Mose left it tied up to the beam. The beam has moved. It is a heavy beam. The rope, the blue rope he tied up the horse with is broken. "He shouldn't be out there," Mose says. I drive down to the next farm and get help. Three Amish kids. It is the first time they have ever ridden in a car. I drive twenty-five miles an hour. I work the electric windows. They are thrilled, crammed with joy. "You drive fast," one of them says. They are all barefoot. So is Mose. We go after the horse. The Amish kids laugh and run, tell jokes, speak Amish. They kid Mose and he kids back. This is fun. This is a game. The horse is important to Mose, vital, and if he does not get it back this will be disastrous. But oh, such fun, such joy! What a day! How could the sky be so blue? For the kids this is a relief from their duties. This does not come often. They laugh and giggle, spit, put hay in their mouths, run after the horse, shout to the horse, shout to Mose who warns them to be careful, this horse will run right through you, this horse is shy of people but at the same time will run right through you. This horse has no fear. Be careful. The kids yelling, giggling, not screaming, not hysterical, know just how to ride joy far enough so that it doesn't turn into fear or anger. This is too good. Let the horse run over them, they think. This is too good. This horse, this meadow, this sky, this day ... this is all too good, and God has allowed us to be here to witness this joy. Oh God, thank you! Thank you!

And I too know that this is so, that this is true. I cannot call this an awakening, but I know it is true, and I thank God. I may not have been granted a perfect timber-fitting experience but I have been granted a perfect horse-losing experience. I do not know if we will ever get the horse back. I expect nothing. It would be good if we did, good for Mose. The tractor farmers around here do not like strange horses roaming through their meadows, scaring their cows. They do not mind shooting horses. We fan out and sweep toward the horse in a line. He looks up at us and moves. "Don't let him get in the woods," Mose says. "If he does we will lose him. We will never get him." The kids in their purple shirts and black pants, bare feet flashing in the grass, run toward the horse. Mose warns them to go slow, to be careful. The horse runs straight for them, black mane against green grass. The children run with their arms outstretched, eager, breathless. We chase the horse into a different meadow. Mose rattles a bucket of oats. The horse is not interested. It will not be easy to catch, this horse. It lets us get close, then runs, stops, looks, waits till we come upon it, runs through us, stops. This is indeed a perfect horse-losing experience! Oh yes.

Incomplete dreams.

THE NIGHT IS SO CLEAR I can see the dust in the sky, the scattered garbage of ice, methane, hydrogen, nitrogen, and rocks that make up the great clutter of the Milky Way. It looks like someone emptied a vacuum cleaner bag on black velvet. Stars, planets, moons, suns, asteroids, comets, vapor trails, chunks and specks from the beginning of time dropped pell mell in the heavens, nothing neat, nothing ordered, nothing that fits in easy categories. It is the spectrum of existence up there, down there, out there, a messy mélange, a great goofy stew thrown through this universe. The moon is a sliver, lost, hidden, so we can see what's been swept under its light. It is a startling sight, shocking to someone who believed the physicists and astronomers and thought there was perfection in space. But nowhere is it written that you must see an ideal, touch faith. It is an uneasy night. I have a hard time getting to sleep. Unpleasant dreams of transplanted organs. I wake up with a shock. I cannot do it. I cannot. This is too much, building a house. It should have been left to experts, those versed in the long chain of materials and labor that must be woven to make this happen. How am I going to cut all the mortises and tenons in time to stay on schedule? What makes me an expert on frost levels and drainage ditches anyway? And I've got all these people (three) working and all this lumber and I don't even have a plan? How stupid! I know how the shell, the frame goes, but after that? I just spent six thousand dollars on doors and windows and I only have a rough idea where they'll go and absolutely no idea how or when I'm going to put them up. Chaos, madness, and folly. Should the rebar have been coated to prevent rusting? Too late, too late. Is the foundation deep enough below the frost line? Too late. How am I going to tie the bents together? No plans for wood joinery between the bents, just nails, spikes, angle irons, and lag bolts. Is that really strong enough? The designer of these frames said the bracing comes from the sheathing you put on. He said you could use 15% of the sheathing area for windows with no structural problems. I am sure we are using more than that. Problems. How is this all going to get done? Sleep. I want all these things to go away.

Harlow insisted he knew more than you and I will ever know. He said this when he was taking a sugar donut out of a cup of milk that had a small amount of coffee in it, and he said it dead on, straight ahead. It is not healthy to come up to this country and tell people you know more than they do, but Harlow said it in a way that made believers out of those he said it to, or at least shut them up. He said this to the waitress at D & B's, a large woman named Shirley who bowled one hundred sixty-eight over the course of a year and had a pair of hands the size of catcher's mitts. "No shit," she said. I think it was only the third time she had said *shit* that week. Harlow told her that what people thought about the Chinese was true. Shirley had no idea what people thought about the Chinese. Her first thought was that a lot of people were thinking things about the Chinese and she hadn't heard about it, and this bothered her because it was her job to know what people were thinking, what was on their minds. You couldn't be a good waitress and not know that. This made her wonder. What was she missing out on? "I don't catch it," she said. Harlow leaned forward and said he knew something else about the Chinese. "I don't follow," Shirley said. Harlow said they fucked with their fingers and ears. "I don't get it," Shirley said.

Waking up.

ABANDON THE WARM BLANKETS in the trailer and throw open the aluminum door. A frosting of ice and near slush, silver-sharp, coats the stubble in the meadow. A low cloud has fallen, a night fog of white/gray, and now squats on the grass. It feels as if I can reach out and touch the fog but wherever I go it remains out of reach. The ice is sharp on my feet. The air bitterly cold around the ankles. A few stars are visible but the clouds are busy and scuttle with a darkling pink against the blue/black of the night. The ground is wet but not mushy, not slimy. Pajamas. Cold below the knees. The ground is icy and wet yet not so icy that bare feet stick to the grass. Steam from my liquid. Ice melts in a widening pool at my feet and as soon as I go in it will freeze in a small circle of a different color. It is refreshing to wake up tired, to be cold, to step on ice and cold damp grass. It wipes the mind clean and focuses the head on the body, on the undulating meadow sheltered in frozen damp. What is out there in the night, sleeping, hunting, killing? Crawling back into the bed clothes with cold wet feet. Waking several hours later and going out again. The sky is barely pink, a rosy mush of ink and blood.

The fog is lower in the meadow, pushing, pushing. The clouds blown away.

Startled by stars. Remembered trees and rocks, sugar maples, pines, hemlock, oak, soft maples, the butts and crests and ridges of rocks rise out of the dark like a damply painted landscape. There are no eyes yet, no muffled sounds, no hushed flap of wings or scuttle of twigs on the forest floor. Day.

Harlow spends most of his time indoors with the heat turned up. He used to smoke but he doesn't smoke now and he used to do more drinking than he does now. He exercises. He took automobile wheels and loaded them with cement and stuck them on the ends of a front axle and spent part of the day inside his trailer with the heat turned up, lifting and sweating. He put concrete in two coffee cans and sawed off a length of broom handle and stuck it in and when he got tired of lifting the front axle, lifted the concrete coffee cans. He wiped the sweat from his eyes and looked out the window to see who was coming down the road. The picture would have been complete if he had turned down the heat and eaten well. He did not. If it came out of a can it was fine with him. And no room was too warm for him. He kept his car heater turned all the way up. He wore underwear, T-shirt, shirt, sweater, vest, liner, and parka, fur-lined, with hood, also lined. His arms and shoulders got big but you never saw them. Exercising, sweating, made him feel gentle, kinder. That's what he told Shirley. She had taken a liking to him. She had always wanted to have a man who knew more than she did but since she was far from stupid she had not found many. He claimed to be one. It made no difference if it was true. Truth was just another casualty in the battle to be alive, and Shirley fought that battle every moment of her life. She had large breasts and large hips and she aimed to make the most of them and never had. She did her drinking at home. She invited him home to drink with her but he would not drink. He did not mind watching her drink. "What do you do if you don't drink?" she asked him. He told her. "I don't think that's normal," she said. Harlow said nothing.

Putting up the bents.

DONALD WELLS HAD THE FARM next to ours. He sold half of his farm to us so that we stood between him and his brother Eldon. Donald and his wife and four kids lived in a two-story house that looked old and flappy but was outrageously lined with bricks. There were two barns, a garage, and two tractors, an Allis-Chalmers and an International Harvester, which he refused to put in the barns. "It's good for them to stay outside," he said. He spoke about these tractors as if he was building their character. In the long run it made sense not to put them in the barns because the barns fell. They didn't fall down as much as they stumbled, as if they had been walking somewhere and just tripped. They sagged so much in the middle, looking like an old broken-backed horse, that it was questionable if they were up or down. Those two old barns were between up and down, both up and down, like most things in life. A heavy windstorm and a heavier snow load did them in and they sagged famously in the middle, old beams pulling out and cracking and the roof splitting apart and reaching up for the wind, and the rain and the hay in the loft fell and then more beams poked out, including one of the beams Mose used to tie his almost-lost horse to.

Harlow and Donald did not get along. One day they had an argument over a line tree. Harlow had just gotten out of the hospital. Donald went back to his house and Harlow went back to his trailer and later when Donald looked out the window Harlow came riding down the road bareback on an old horse. He was holding a shotgun. "Let's get the hell out of here," Donald said, and he rushed the wife and kids into the cellar. Harlow road his horse into Donald's barn and pointed the shotgun at one of his cows and pulled the trigger. Donald never left the barn door shut; you just had to open it again. Harlow rode out and looked around and then looked up at the sky and decided it was a one-cow-killing day and rode off. When Donald came up from the cellar and saw what had happened he called the sheriff. "Harlow's been skipping his medicine again," the sheriff said. Years later Donald fell down, like his barns, and couldn't get up and went to the hospital where he died. His kids were grown up and married and one of them was in Vietnam and came back and was angry with everything. Donald's wife lived in the house for a while and then went to a home for the retired. She still had this farm she couldn't sell because she could never get the title cleared so she came back to live in the old house with her daughter and her daughter's kids and her daughter's husband who had a part of him on the inside that was broke. Everything seemed to be broke on that farm except the two old tractors, which were just rusty but when oiled up and the ignition wires replaced and a new battery put in and new tires put on and the wheels re-welded and the front end worked on some and a new distributor put in and the gunk cleaned out of the carburetor and a new head gasket put on, worked fine. Every spring

Donald used to take us out to find morels, and he always knew where they were and now there's no one who does. He was a stubborn man, but I miss him, I do. The barns are old and gray. They look like four barns, or four what-might-be-barns. The middle halves are just about gone, sucked out, except for a pile of beams sitting on the ground, sticking up, showing the old adz marks and the mortise pockets for tenons that have long since been pulled out. We used one of those old beams to hold up the floor joists.

Donald's been away for some years now, and when I was away for almost a week and came back I found that Mose and Andy had cut the remaining mortises and tenons and assembled the three remaining bents and that they had them piled up on the deck in the order that they should be put up. Without me there they had done three times the work that had been done when I was there. I looked at the joints. Not bad. Not perfect, not very good, but not bad. One of the twenty-foot beams was rounded where it sat in the shoulder. The log had tapered into its 8-by-12 at nineteen and a half feet so the 12 didn't go out the full eight inches but only seven inches or so and the 8 didn't run down the full twelve inches but only eleven near the outside. I was not going to cut another timber. It would go up like that. The beam drill press was set up and the Briggs & Stratton pull started, and the heavy steel bit chewed its way through the timber, coughing up curling scraps of wood. Hardwood pins were inserted to secure the mortise-and-tenon joints. We brace it with a plank and drive the backhoe around to one side of the deck and wrap a chain around the middle of the bent. The problem here is to lift it up gently without banging these huge timbers against the deck or having the posts skid off the deck. The best way to raise a bent is by hand, by many hands, the way the Amish do it. This way you get the strength to have it tipped up and the slowness and gentleness that only comes with doing something by hand. Hands tell you when to push, how to push, where to push, and when and how to stop. Even with a crane jerking a heavy bent skyward, it is hands that must guide it down, place the posts in the correct position. The backhoe lifts, the bucket rattling and jerking, the chain tightens and yanks, and the bent is lifted, slowly swinging in the air, the wood against the sky, the bent dangling over the deck. It must be lowered, slowly, slowly. The backhoe bounces it off the deck. This is the best it can do. We nail two boards on the post sides, about seven feet up, and with the posts resting on the deck, push on the boards until the bent is perpendicular, or nearly so. We want the posts resting exactly at the corner of the deck so the sheathing can overlap the deck. It is impossible to get this much accuracy with a backhoe, so we take a sledgehammer and slowly pound them over. Dan, Mose's brother, has a better idea. He attaches a nailer near the bottom and uses a crowbar to lift and "walk" the leg of the bent over. A final tap puts it just where we want it. I stand back. The first bent is up, braced, nailed to the deck.

Harlow wanted to know why he skidded down the road on his head and why the propane had blown him in the air. He'd been through the Korean War and come out mostly whole, except for a little frostbite on his fingers and some upset because he put a bayonet through the belly of a Chinese soldier. He thought maybe the Chinese soldier wanted to talk to him, wanted to tell him something. He thought about a lot of things when he went down the highway on his head and he had thought a lot more when he was in the air from the propane. He thought maybe there was some explaining he should do. Soldiers are like that, but Harlow didn't think of himself as a soldier and he realized that even soldiers didn't think of themselves as soldiers. No one did. When he was in Korea he realized how much Korea was like upper New York state, the northern part near the St. Lawrence River. It was cold, startling country. The faces on the people were windswept and they walked leaning into the wind. Night came like thunder and the days blazed or drizzled or sat on you with a thick fog. The trees were alike. In both places he had seen someone hang himself from a tree and in both places there was nothing he could do about it. People spoke the same way too. He had trouble understanding them. Even on the hottest day he could feel a chill in the air, a re-alignment of air currents. Both places were rich in plants, and both grew ginseng. Once, during a huge battle near Seoul when the Chinese swept over the hills like cattle, never stop-ping even when they were mercilessly machine-gunned, Har-low thought he was back in the valley near the Oswegatchie River and that the Chinese had swept down from Canada. He wanted to put down his rifle and turn to his buddies on the line and tell them, "It's OK, it's OK, they're only Canadians." His father had left him the farm but by that time it wasn't much of a farm and he sold it and moved into a trailer down the road and bought several internal combustion engines, which he had taken apart and scattered around the acre and a half the trailer sat on. He played golf under par on a miniature golf course and exercised with concrete and steel. He collected feed sacks and piled them underneath his trailer. He never ex-plained anything, not a single thing, not even in school. He believed there was nothing he could ever explain. But he liked to hear other people explain. He watched when the state in-troduced beavers up in the north country (they had been ex-tirpated around the turn of the century) and watched the beavers multiply ferociously and dam up all the low fields so the farmers complained and the state brought in shotguns and dynamite and tried to wipe them out again, but failed, not being as rapacious, as avaricious, as efficient as earlier hunters. When Eldon died Harlow refused to eat meat. That was about all Eldon ate. He liked Eldon and after his funeral got the idea that Eldon lived on cereal and milk. Harlow thought Eldon had some secret he should know about, that Eldon had a secret he kept from the rest of the county. Maybe he did. Maybe Eldon's secret was this: *When I am gone no one will remember me.*

But if that was his secret, he was wrong. I will remember him.

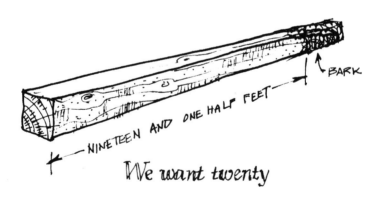

NINETEEN AND ONE HALF FEET

BARK

We want twenty

Attaching the bents.

Now THERE ARE FOUR BENTS PROPPED UP on the deck, truncated Hs twelve feet high by twenty feet long, stuck up at intervals of ten feet with boards diagonally nailed to the bent and the deck. The bents need to be attached to each other and the joists that do the attaching will be the underpinning for the second floor. The best way to do this is with further mortises and tenons; each beam running parallel to the deck would protrude tenons at both ends, which then fit into mortises carefully dug into the post of the bent. But this takes more time and more money than I have. Several experienced timber framers gnawing furiously at the wood like human beavers, working with a chisel and slick to produce a tight joint into which the wood fits snugly and evenly, and of course, at a right angle, would be the best solution. There is one school that suggests using angle iron and lag bolts for this attachment. Not as "pure" but quick and neat. Not as strong either. For some reason, this solution offends me. Another school suggests toenailing the beams to the post. This solution horrifies traditionalists, but this is what we do. Dan and Mose sit across the beams and while I steady the connecting

Hammer. Nail. Wood.

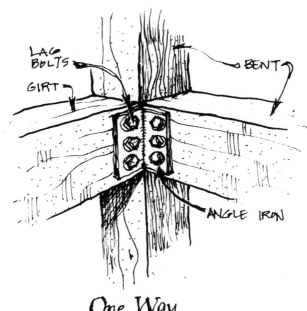

One Way

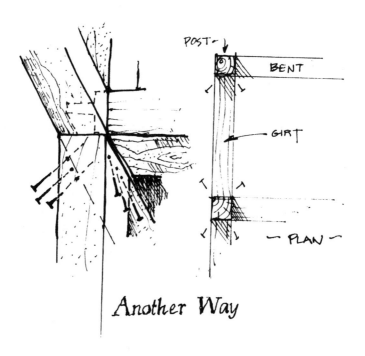

Another Way

80

beam in place, they pound. Bam! Yellow lumber against blue sky, black-trousered legs dangling in the air, the silver flash of hammers and nails. This is how we do it. This is how it gets done. Now the frame is up, the bents connected. All that's left are the plates that fit on top of the posts and form the foundation for the roof rafters. These are 8-by-8s, and the suggestion from one school is that we rest each one on half the cross-section of the post and then drill a hole fourteen inches long and put some rebar through. Again, this bothers me. Driving large pieces of steel through the end of a timber risks splitting the timber, even if the holes are predrilled. Especially if the pieces of rebar cross each other. We decide to half-lap the 8-by-8 plates and nail them in with large nails. Bottom first, and then top to the bottom. Argument could be made that this also risks splitting, but the nail is much shorter than the rebar, and less holes are made in the post. It may not be the most elegant solution, but it works. I hope.

Emile Thiebault drove a 1958 white flatbed truck piled high with immense amounts of scrap steel and iron. It was all metal, mostly, except for bits of plastic signs, crankcase oil, wood to brace the engine blocks, and PCB insulation from old Niagara Mohawk electric generators. It was engine blocks and propeller blades from St. Lawrence Seaway ships, transformer housings, rolls of copper wire, stationary engines, Buick bumpers, Studebaker transmissions, DeSoto rear ends, and leaf springs as wide as fire hoses, delicately balanced on the flatbed. A mountain of steel and iron. Tie it down? Why tie it down? Suppose a Buick engine block rolls off? You can't do much damage to that engine block. But if you are talking about a highway menace, either you are talking about Henry Langer, who owned a diner on Rt. 11, which he turned into a farm implement store and who would occasionally steal cars and make them go faster than they were ever intended to go, and the only way he could be caught is when he ran out of gas, or Emile. Now if it was Henry the solution was easy. Give him lithium. If it was Emile that was something different. Emile had a God-given right to put whatever he wanted to on the back of his flatbed truck and drive as fast as he wanted to. Interfere with that and you were interfering with the American way of life. He wouldn't take drugs. Henry had taken drugs and you saw what it did to him. Drugs were part of the plot. Emile thought communists lived in his left nostril and reported what he did to Moscow. Now from that it might sound like it was easy to dismiss Emile, but it was not.

There's more to Emile. He and Skyler owned the two junkyards in the area. Skyler had the more modern junkyard and had more cars. He had all his cars stacked neatly and was more up to date, had them entered in a computer, but Skyler was a dreamer. Emile, he couldn't afford to be a dreamer. His junkyard looked like a very messy farm, as if he had tried and failed at several things: running a trailer park, selling used batteries and tires, alternative-energy windmills, and turntable cow stations like they have on those superfarms in California. Skyler is dead now. He died with a smile on his face. Emile will never have a smile on his face.

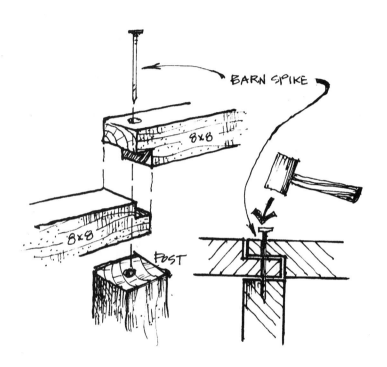

BARN SPIKE

8x8

8x8

POST

Junkyard ball.

Ray Decker was the best pitcher we had in junkyard ball. His specialty was a soft floater that eased over the plate, flicking bits of grease and grit and wobbling in midair just before the strike zone. Sometimes it just got too heavy and dropped at the plate, making a kind of right angle, like a Stillson wrench. That was a delicious pitch. Ray liked to annoy Skyler with that pitch. With a close game, one hundred twenty-two to one-thirty, and Skyler up to bat and Ray knew he had to not only get Skyler out but also annoy him, make him mad enough so that for the remainder of the game, whether it was a four-inning game or a fourteen-inning game, he couldn't hit.

Skyler complained about that pitch. Skyler had the junkyard outside Heuvelton. He was a low, squat man who managed to get considerable heft into the bat. He was one of our better hitters when he didn't stop to complain. Skyler would rather complain than play junkyard ball, and that certainly qualified him for our league. Most of the people who play junkyard ball like to complain, or do something else that gets in the way of the game. But really, for a fact, hardly anything can get in the way of our brand of ball.

People everywhere have tried to stop us. We got a letter once from the Commissioner of Baseball.

There is no season for junkyard ball. That is, every season, any season. We even play in the summer. We play nine to a team, or eight or seven, once twelve. We play all men, all women, all men and women, all men and women and dogs. Dogs are encouraged to play. In point of fact a dog playing is one of the more encouraging sights in junkyard ball, and we can certainly use all the encouragement we can get.

We always play with a bat and ball. The bat looks like a bat and the ball does too but the ball can be any size, any weight, any shape. We do any kind of pitching too. Any kind.

We had a woman softball pitcher come in once and clean our clocks. Then we set up a rule against her. We have certain variable rules, and certain invariable ones. That is, we have one invariable rule. We play ball in junkyards. The league is Skyler's junkyard in Heuvelton, Ernie's junkyard in Rensselaer Falls, Scote's junkyard in Potsdam, and Emile's in Gouverneur. Several bigger junkyards in Albany and Syracuse wanted to get in but we ruled against them. We could see where that was headed. You don't want to make too big a thing out of this.

Junkyard ball is nasty ball. Skyler and Emile both have teams, have sort of teams. Sometimes they have nine on a team, sometimes men, sometimes adults. They have this great affection for each other because they, along with Scote, Ernie, and others, are the Aborigines of commerce. Junkyard owners are despised, the spit-upon of small businessmen; they band together out of necessity.

But on the playing field Skyler and Emile hated each other. With a vengeance. It was a marvelous sort of hate, a hate that flowed freely and easily, and it was a wonderful sight to see on the field. For example if Skyler showed up with two players and those two players formed a bond and vowed to hate Emile's players and Emile showed up with ten players, primed to hate Skyler's, and if they got on the field and saw the inconsistency in numbers, they would reformulate the two teams until they had six and six, and the hate too would reformulate, the new six hating the other six. It was wonderful to see.

Even the best of friends would forgo their friendship and enter into a new bond of hate (or a new bond of friendship if they happened to be on a team with someone they hated).

The rules in junkyard ball are somewhat relaxed, though if you know baseball you would recognize junkyard baseball. Harlow overstepped these rules when he took a baseball bat to the pitcher. This brought the game to a complete halt, though there are many things that bring the game to a halt, and the rules were questioned. We agreed that bats were not allowed to be used on pitchers, only umpires. The only thing you can do to a pitcher is kick and punch. Throwing of metal objects is not allowed, though we relaxed that rule for Ray Decker once when he pitched a beautiful game with a small armature, copper-wound.

For our World Series we go to Scote's in Potsdam. Scote is quite obliging. He cleared a couple rows of rusting Brockway Diesels and moved thirty-seven salt-frosted aluminum laundry cages and put up plastic snow fences. The home-run area was behind them, where the Niagara-Mohawk generators with PCB insulation are stacked. Ball goes in there, we just leave it alone.

One winter day Decker pitched a near perfect game. He got tagged only once, by Mary Malone, who hit the ball right in the middle of the PCBs. She said it wasn't a ball she hit, and Ray admitted that. Mary was going out with Bob Malone, no relation, and she learned about the game because Bob was a junkyard junkie, always searching for eternal motion springs for the machinery he builds in Pope Mills. You can see the stuff stacked in his front yard from the highway. He once sold a carburetor to General Motors. A Miracle Carburetor. Course they wouldn't use it. He wasn't much of a player though.

We don't have uniforms. We could have uniforms. The big aluminum company in Massena offered to suit up the winners of the Junkyard Series, but we've always had a hard time determining just who wins any game we play. Besides, it just wouldn't look right in the field. Guys in Carhart canvas suits, Amish in black with straw hats, farmers in striped overalls, mill hands in jeans and wool shirts would have to watch a bunch of prissies prance out in baseball uniforms. That would rile us. We tend to get ugly when riled.

A big-league player came down once to look us over. He was Triple A, from Binghamton. He never did say a word to us when he left.

Sometimes we play for a week, seven consecutive days, sometimes we go for months without playing. That's why you'll never find our schedules up in any of the bars, though word gets out when we're ready to play. We're like termites that way. Everyone just knows when we're going to play.

Our best game, the best game of the season, if you want to call last year a season, was not at Scote's but Emile's. Emile's junkyard goes uphill. It never stops going uphill and the same goes for the playing field. He doesn't use snow fences like Scote. Emile has whatever Emile has to make a fence: milk separators, barbed wire snagged and rusty, gang plows, salt spreaders, pushed-over flatbeds. The ball at Emile's responds to this uphill. The fences are moved in. Playing field doesn't need to be as big. You get a good hit and the ball just whistles right off the bat and starts to climb, rocket ready. But soon that ball commences to realize what it has to do to get over the fence. It's got to go uphill, keep going uphill. That is some climb on that field, and the ball will get tired and just give up. What the hell. It suddenly drops, like Ray's special pitches.

Ray's floater doesn't work going downhill. There's only one kind of pitch on Emile's field, and that's a fast ball, a triple-fast ball. Emile's got something in the ground that seems to attract baseballs, plus that and going downhill just naturally accelerates the pitch. By the time it reaches the plate that ball is screaming. Now you're going to say: why not turn the field around? But you don't know junkyard ball. We've got our rules. Funny thing is, the situation is more advantageous for batters than for pitchers. Reason is you never know where a hit ball will drop. And reason is when you throw a ball downhill it tends to run in a groove, at least it does at Emile's, and once the batter finds that groove he's got a good piece of that ball.

This was late September, a strange time for us to be playing but there you have it. That day the weather was just about as perfect as weather can be. Greens and golds of the trees, the sky so blue it hurts, and the blacks, reds, and yellows from the pools of oil, the rusty combines, and the fungus growing out of the milk separators.

Ray Decker was pitching and Babs Decker was up to bat. Ray loves that woman, and Babs him too, but pitching to her is another story. It takes two of Ray to make one of Babs. And she can arm wrestle him solid to the ground, though she won't do it when company is around.

It was the top half of the fifteenth. The score was zero to zero. Babs at bat and the Decker's dog Software was on second. Software was not playing second base. Software was on second base, a base runner, and that damned dog was some base runner. Software would watch the hit ball. If it was caught he wouldn't run. If it was not, he ran. Don't tell me dogs are stupid.

Ray was trying to spook that dog. The dog was his and he kept looking over his shoulder at it, yelling at it to come here, to sit, to lie down, to beg. But let me say this in defense of the dog. When that dog plays junkyard ball his mind, what little there is of it, is on the game. You can't ask for more than that.

Ray is disgusted with the dog but he gives up and turns around to face Babs. The dog gets ready to run. He knows Babs. Ray thinks he will brush her back from the plate, just to let her know whose game it is.

The first pitch goes clear behind her head and almost knocks off her MacAdams Cheese cap. Babs works in cheese curl. She heat seals.

The second pitch—well, that second pitch is something you rarely see. I have never seen a corkscrew pitch, nor has anyone else when you really get to questioning them. But this pitch, tell me they're not putting some strange stuff in the ground with funny currents that go back and forth very quickly. Emile claims not to know anything about it. He says that stuff was buried years ago before they had all those regulations about where you put waste.

We will forget the second pitch.

The third pitch, that was right in the shooter's groove. Babs swings. She hits. Software is sitting but not to worry. That dog can get up faster than any dog I know. He's got his head up looking at the ball. He turns his head as the ball sails over. He keeps looking. The ball keeps going.

Did you ever see a dog look at a ball? I mean really look at a ball? That is a marvelous sight, something wondrous. Software has this look on his face, insofar as dogs can get looks on their faces, that says . . . I guess wisdom comes closest to it.

The dog seems to know something about the ball. The dog seems to know something about the ball that we don't know, and that ball just keeps going, going uphill too, so you know how hard that ball is hit.

But the dog will not get up. The dog is trained to get up and run with a well-hit ball, a ball that drops somewhere no one can catch it, this time not in the PCBs like at Scote's, but back in the weeds, a kind of weed that seems to thrive around junk-yards.

The ball keeps going and going. It never stops. The dog does not get up because he does not see the ball fall, and Babs, she's rounding first and having a fit. You see the rules are quite clear in junkyard ball.

You can't overtake a base runner. I don't care what. And Software, that was one well-trained dog. He was simply wait-ing for the ball to drop, like he had been taught.

I would call that the apotheosis of junkyard ball. So far.

The government trees.

YOU CAN DRIVE for an hour through the back country and run across corn and cropped pasture and meadows overgrown to gnarled brush and staggered, stunted trees of just about every description, but within that hour you will surely come across rows of pine trees, string straight, all the same height, evenly spaced like paper clips in mud. How in the ...! You brake the car to a halt. How did this ...? How did these trees ...?

W.P.A.

Men were out of work and trees needed to be planted. No one apologized for planting trees in those days. This was right after the dust storms in the thirties. You didn't have to make a case for the importance of trees—for the soil, for the water, for the air, for the well-being of the crops that were nestled in between the battalions of trees. These pines now look so comforting, so regular. They are about seventy-five feet tall, belly-thick, six feet apart. Many of the men who planted those trees are dead, or will be dead shortly. As boys Donald and Eldon planted trees. It wasn't much money, even then. But their father was grateful for the money and so were the boys. Now they're not boys, not even men. They're gone, but they've left us those trees. Pines don't let much grow underneath them. A thick coat of needles on the ground drives out the underbrush and makes it easy to walk among them, and they're not bashful about their smell. Those pines are straight. I have yet to see one of them crooked. You can find them planted all over, the areas randomly chosen, like joy.

You can find joy in lots of places. Old hardware stores, the kind that would never put a pot or pan in the window. When I walk into a real hardware store in the north country it just takes my breath away. There is always a wall filled with hammers, the hammers all angled to pound invisible nails. Those hickory handles and drop-forged steel heads call to me. I want to take some home though I already have a dozen hammers. Saws. The shiny flat, whiplike blade, the bifurcated row of teeth, like tiny carpenter ants who take instruction, and the handles on those saws, my goodness! Those handles make you want to hold on to that saw forever. The arch on that grip feels so good, the wood dusky and deep, the seductive curve of the big brass rivets that anchor it to the saw blade so enticing. Levels! Don't get me going on levels. I love the long ones, six feet, dark polished wood with the shimmering green vials nestled in the center, the whole thing trimmed in metal, with a groove down the middle so you can spend your day knowing what to do with your thumb. Nails. I have never seen a bad-looking nail. Not the way you can see an ugly screwdriver. All of these are new tools, just waiting for you to put personality into them so that fifty years from now someone else can appreciate them.

At this moment I do not follow the distinction between managed and unmanaged joy, between trees and hardware stores, between sunsets and a gorgeous chisel that balances perfectly in the palm of your hand, the steel blade reaching out like the edge of a canyon, hawk-sharp, to cut into wood, the handle of the chisel fitting so well you can hold it and instantly know how good everything is.

I am intemperate and immature about this, too enthusiastic, not critical enough. When you are young you are enthusiastic without knowing what to hook that enthusiasm to, and when you are old you forget what you were enthusiastic about while still being able to keep that enthusiasm. It is in-between the two, where most of us are, that you stand the greatest danger of losing your enthusiasm.

Harlow got to know the county jail pretty well, never less than ten days but never more than thirty. He was calm in spurts. He was usually calm when he saw a uniform, calmer when he saw several uniforms, and he was always calm when he was surrounded by steel bars. He was the calmest man anyone had ever seen in jail. He took to jails. Some people are like that. In jail Harlow rested, gathering up the energy he would need for his next spurt. Steel bars soothed him, made him feel lavish and forgiving.

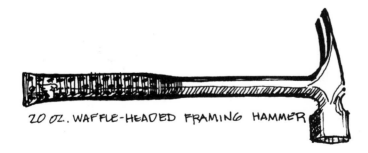

20 OZ. WAFFLE-HEADED FRAMING HAMMER

Where to look for joy.

A DRAIN PIPE THAT RAN DIAGONALLY down and across the end of our barn had separated, allowing water from the roof to empty at midpoint. The side of the barn that took the water was gray, the stain fan-shaped. The more it rained the sooner that wood might rot. How to repair it. Repair on a farm is never a simple process. You must go through every step of the repair and imagine how you will make the repair and from this calculate all the tools you will need. If you make this repair on a ladder you do not want to be going up and down that ladder, or driving back and forth into town for the trivial. The drive from the city was eight hours, in a friend's car with a leaky transmission. I was worried all the way up, thinking I would get stuck in the Adirondacks, and even after I arrived I couldn't shake the worry from my mind. A good part of the day was still left. The sky was sparkling. Climbing up the long ladder to the side of the barn where the leader had separated I felt uneasy. How was I going to make this repair? What if I fell? Does it make sense to drive sixteen hours up and back just to make repairs on a drain leader on a barn? What if wind pushes the ladder over? The end of the top leader was supposed to be pounded in to fit inside the bottom leader. How could I pound that, on a ladder? How could I make a nail hole in these pieces of metal? How could I reattach them so they would stay in place? How? How?? I do not remember making that repair, though I must have. I do remember something else though. The sky opened. I saw something. I saw how miraculous everything was. Everything just was.

The roof goes up.

FORTY-THREE DEGREES IS THE ANGLE at which snow on a roof begins to slip. This varies with the composition of the roofing material and the kind of snow, but in general this is the slipping angle. It is also the angle at which aggregate in a pile will fall rather than build up.

The original plan called for fourteen-foot-long 4-by-8 roof rafters, four feet on center, half lapped at the apex and pegged. The result is a forty-three-degree angle. At this length 4-by-8s are heavy and rather expensive, so we decided to go with 2-by-8s, sixteen feet long to give the roof some overhang, and to run them two feet on center. This gives less strength, but we'll use collar ties and other supports. Using the edges of the deck as the width of our roof sill, we laid out our first rafter on the deck, and when we were satisfied that the rafter would indeed fit on the roof, nailed a triangular support plate at the top and a 2-by-8 collar tie a third of the way from the top, to provide additional bracing for the rafter and also as a grid for insulation. Roof insulation is critical, especially here, where the temperature can drop to forty below. Then we nailed blocks to the deck, which formed a template for the roof rafters, and

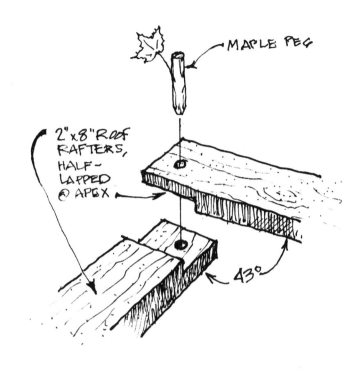

MAPLE PEG

2"x8" ROOF RAFTERS, HALF-LAPPED @ APEX

43°

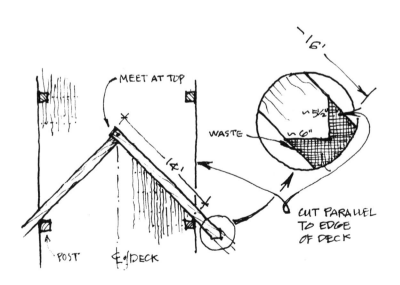

MEET AT TOP

POST

℄ of DECK

WASTE

6'

5½'

6"

CUT PARALLEL TO EDGE OF DECK

Hammer. Nail. Wood.

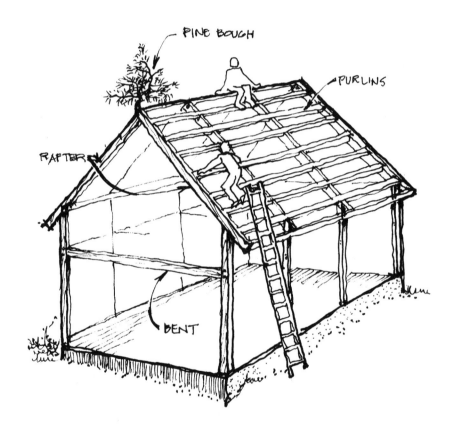

PINE BOUGH

PURLINS

RAFTER

BENT

The Original Plan

began our work. Raising a roof rafter suggests some foresight because the rafter is longer than the width of the house, i.e. longer than the bents. Talk about a tight fit! The rafters that will become the end of the roof can be raised upside down, and raised high enough so that as the inverted V reaches the top of the sill plate it can be pushed a bit higher until it can hang upside down. Then it is flipped over, carefully, and "walked" into place. Rafters further in must be raised upside down and then turned, one end tilted slightly to clear the width of the house, and then lifted to the top, flipped, and walked into place. This must be done consecutively, from one end to the other end, otherwise you run into a mess in the middle, trying to raise rafters with not enough clearance. Of course if you have a crane, forget this. Take your giant's hand and just plop them in place.

The rafter ends are handed up to Dan and I who stand on opposite sills. Then the apex is raised. While we hold these in place, the apex is raised with a long pole, Clyde pushing on the bottom and Mose up at the apex of an adjoining rafter, pulling and grunting. Once you have several up you can use a pulley to raise the others. We work until the inevitable happens and we realize we've left too little space to maneuver. Bents and connecting timbers are in the way. This is a good time to look at the sky. Somehow, twisted, pulled perpendicular to the roof, the remaining rafters go up. A pine bough gets nailed on the top for good luck. When all the rafters are up the purlins are nailed on. These tie the rafters together and provide additional support for the roof. You can scramble up the roof using the purlins as a ladder and see what you will see out your second story window. The delightful, the objectionable, the unavoidable, the surprising . . . what you couldn't see from the first floor you now see from the roof, more or less of it depending on how far up or down the roof you are. I ease down to the ground and walk back to look. Oh, . . . the beauty of it. Why does this have to be covered?

For a while Harlow thought he should live in air. He climbed up to the roof of his trailer and lugged his stained and rusty concrete-and-steel weights up. He decided he needed a convertible. He cut off the top half of a Chevrolet Biscayne sedan he bought from Skyler. He slept on the roof of the trailer, except in the spring during black-fly season. He drove a logging truck for a company down in Long Lake, driving with the windows open so the great swill of summer would empty on his face and when winter came kept the same windows open but the heater turned on. It was a good job and paid well. One day a logging chain snapped and he watched the logs tumble down a hill just outside Old Forge. It was some sight, those logs going down that hill. Some rolled, bounced and rolled, but a few walked down the hill, just stood on end and hopped down. He had never seen logs hopping down a hill. It was a masterly sight. It was an unnerving sight. Logs bounced into trees, bending trees, cracking trees, filling the air with the sounds of a celestial bowling alley. Bits of bark, gouges, wood chips. Underbrush swept flat. He drove Shirley in the topless Biscayne down to Old Forge to see the temple of logs gathered at the bottom of a ravine. She spent most of the drive trying to hold her hair in place and then gave up. She did not know what to make of the logs, did not know if there was anything to make of them, but no longer wondered why Harlow had driven her down to see the fallen logs. They had a picnic of hard-boiled eggs and Swiss cheese on the logs and then climbed back up the hill to the car. It was the first of many trips. Harlow searched out any disaster in the area, plane crash, car wreck, farming accident, and if there was anything left of it on Shirley's day off they drove to the scene of the

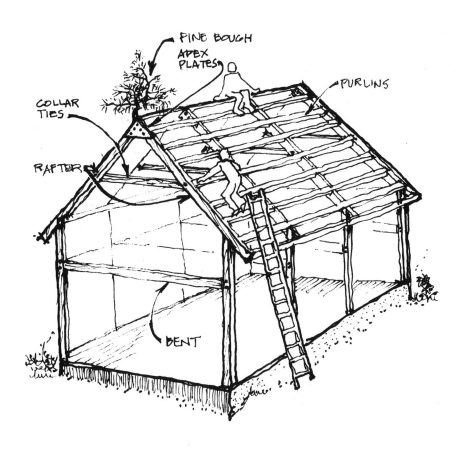

PINE BOUGH

APEX PLATES

PURLINS

COLLAR TIES

RAFTER

BENT

The Revised Plan

disaster. Shirley had no idea what she was supposed to do until Harlow told her. She had a long scarf she wore over her hair and ear muffs under the scarf. He told her to take off the scarf and the ear muffs and listen. "Listen to what?" she asked. "Listen," he said. "You can hear it. Listen." She listened for five, ten minutes. Harlow waited until she had a certain look on her face.

When things fall, burn, slide.

USUALLY IT HAPPENS IN SPRING, after a wet, heavy snow and then rain. The weather is warm but not warm enough to melt the snow, which acts like a sponge and sucks in water. Tons of water sit on the roof until the roof can no longer support this swimming pool. With a loud pop, a crack that can be heard for miles, the roof settles in the middle like an old horse that can't get up anymore but keeps trying. What is inside the barn is soon not. The barn becomes two smaller barns, or one and a half barns, depending upon how you look at it, if the barn is still up enough so you can look at it. A barn is marvelous space, space for wood, tools, tractors, animals, hay, and most marvelous of all, space for nothing, neck-bending space that goes up for dozens of feet with nooks and rafters for rats, cats, pigeons, bats, snakes, toads, turtles, swallows, wasps, bees, and dozens of other species. A broken barn is a violation of this space, a sad crack in the system of farming. You want to put a broken barn out of its misery, you want to shoot a broken barn.

Fires come quickly. Wood is plentiful here and wood stoves are common and most buildings are made from wood. Fire is quite democratic about what wood it burns. When a barn goes up it's tragic but when a house goes up more so. By the time the fire is phoned in, assuming it can be phoned in, and by the time the fire engine reaches the house, most of the damage, most of the tragedy has been done. It is not pleasant to come upon burned bodies in charred timbers or snow.

Rarely, but sometimes, a building decides to move itself. It does not like the ground it is on and the ground returns the favor by going soft, shoving earth and mud on the upside of what is a downhill-facing building. When the building decides it has had enough of this it moves. A mud slide has come to pass. This is rare, but spectacular enough to be an occasion. It is particularly intriguing if you can be there to watch.

Disasters are temporary. They only last for years. Henry Langer of Rt. 11 claimed to be a prophet. But his prophecy only extended several miles on both sides of Richville, just off Rt. 11. He prophesied in the basement of the Methodist church. He said that within several years huge trucks would come carrying large spools of wire and the men who drove those trucks would not speak any known English language but a long forgotten biblical language and that soon after they came a giant cross fifty feet tall would be erected on the side of the hill outside Richville and on both sides of the giant cross would be smaller crosses, ten feet tall. He said the large cross would be made of wood and once a year the top would burn and a boy would come to preach in front of the cross, speaking in a language they did not understand, but when they went to sleep that night they would understand what he said and they would wake up feeling wonderful and hike across the country setting up crosses. Several months later men from the south came in pickup trucks to lay a natural gas line. They spent most of their time complaining about the cold weather. Farmers sold them hay and Harlow helped pack it around the pipe until he hit one of the southerners over the head with a shovel.

That was the last real job Harlow had. Except for driving around in the Biscayne and looking for disasters he didn't do much of anything. He told Shirley good-bye and she said where are you going and he said nothing. She asked him what he was going to do. He said he was going to watch things. What things she asked. Everything, he said, it all needs watching. He watched them lay the gas line and he watched them put in the new bridge near De Peyster and stood on the other side of the Oswegatchie when they shored up the river bank under the post office in Heuvelton. There was a sort of balance between these projects and his disasters. They canceled out, or maybe one made the other possible.

People were bored with Henry Langer. They just got fed up with him.

How fast is a running foot?

BUILDING A HOUSE used to be a sacred undertaking. Before selecting the site, cutting the wood, one asked forgiveness, one asked a blessing. Grace was an inherent feature in building, as it was in other tasks. One lived by grace and through grace, and the acts and deeds of a lifetime contributed or took away from that grace. Now I think about what we've put up. It is a beautiful construction in wood, but too late I remember that I did not ask permission to build, did not kneel down on the site, did not apologize to the trees. This may seem silly, but it is the silly and sacred that inform our lives, give joy and energy, spirit and meaning. When I think about what I have truly remembered, the things that warmly informed my heart, they have all come to me by grace. They are often silly and sometimes monumental, but a spirit runs through them. They are often preceded by an extreme amount of work and energy, but in themselves they are effortless, easy. They flow through you. You are fortunate to be there, to witness, to be the physical body through which they take place. You need to do a lot of work to get yourself to a place where you are responsible for what happens by not causing it to happen. I did not build this house. Yet this house would not have been built without me. But "I" hardly built it. This is more than just recognizing that many people are involved in putting up a house. This is the grace of building. I hope I have asked for blessing, cherished what should be cherished. I hope my words find favor. I hope my building is solid. All I can do is hope. It is hardly "my" building.

Putting a roof on it.

UNCOVERED, A POST-AND-BEAM STRUCTURE has a threaded substantiality about it. It seems a shame to cover it. The large timbers, locked into each other, framed against the sky, provide both the security and openness one needs. They are complete unto themselves. They secure the space but do not dominate it, define but do not intrude. Sky and air are the perfect cover. Large timbers have been liberated from trees and need to feel the air, rain, sun. But a shelter needs skin to protect, warm, cover, to keep things out. Usually a roof goes on first, if for no other reason than to keep you dry while you put on the rest of the covering. If you are not using prefab roofing—large, heavy, insulated pieces that function as a top hat—the choice is shingles or tin. Tin roofs—actually galvanized metal—come in long, wide strips and also come with a cheap image. Or used to. Now you can get them enameled, the color baked on. A shingled roof needs boards or plywood completely covering the whole roof since each shingle is nailed on. A tin roof needs only rafters spaced to match the width of the roof's metal sections. We decided to put on a red tin roof. (There goes the neighborhood.) Nick is up on the ridge and Brendan climbs up the purlins while I stay down by the roof sills and Bob, on the ground, hands up the roofing. The nails are galvanized and come with a small rubber washer that seals the space between the nailhead and the hole you make pounding through the tin. Nailing through tin is one of life's sweeter experiences. Attack the nailhead and nothing happens, except that you dent the tin, and invariably, without a doubt, absolutely, bang your finger. Only after having sufficiently smashed your finger will the nail go through the tin. Taking your fury out on the tin will only leave you with a crippled, leaky roof. And it is not nice to throw hammers off the roof.

Emile used to do that with open-end wrenches. He'd be driving down the highway with his mound of junk and spot a communist by the side of the road. Out would go the wrench, spinning, smash into that communist. Skyler did not believe in communists. I once bought some cable, turnbuckles, cinch nuts, and wire loops from Skyler to tighten up a barn beam that was pulling apart and threatening to topple over the barn. Skyler looked up in his computer and told me just where that cable was lying, just where on the ground it would be. I always marveled that about him. You would go into his office and there was this mess: dirt floor, kerosene heater that periodically caught fire. His office was in a trailer that had the floor chopped out. I never asked him why he chopped the floor out. Skyler's wife lived on sugar. He wore cowboy hats. You would think a man who wore cowboy hats in the east would have swagger and dash, but Skyler didn't. Most junkyard dealers come from another planet. But Skyler, well, he was the gentlest junkyard dealer I ever knew. He didn't even have a junkyard dog. He grew flowers. He listened to bad music. He listened to Harlow.

How the weather gets your attention.

Nature writing is done by people indoors and all books written about the weather are written indoors by people who are very glad they are indoors. Weather is not sun. When you have sun you have no weather. Weather is water. Water in the clouds or water in the sky or water in the ground or water somewhere between, but real weather is all three, and when you have wind and clouds and rain and snow and fog, all five and the combinations of all five (ice and hail and mud and sleet and everything that goes along with that) then you have yourself some real weather. This is nothing to rhapsodize over. If anyone tells you there is glory in this you know they are very warm when they say this, inside, dry, and are very likely having a cup of coffee or herb tea with honey and lemon. Up north, real weather can be debilitating. If you have to work outside in real weather, and most people up north do, if you are lucky you will be uncomfortable and if you are unlucky you may get killed and if you are very unlucky you could get maimed. Machinery and real weather do not mix, and most outside work in the north is done with machinery. The only people who do not use machinery outside are those people who do not make their living outside, who are outside as a hobby, a pastime, a lark, people who can hardly wait to rush inside and write about being outside. These are Nature Writers. People like me.

It is depressing to be outside in the cold and fog, especially if there is snow and mud and the sun is long gone, vanished. Being rained on in the snow is also unpleasant, as is being snowed on in the rain, especially if you are doing something that requires that you do not wear gloves, or requires that you wear gloves but the gloves are cold and wet, or requires that you wear waterproof gloves but your hands are hot and sticky inside the gloves from the sweat and the horrible material used to insulate these gloves. There is nothing more ghastly than trudging through snow when it rains and discovering that your boots are turning the snow into mud. The only thing worse than that is seeing a dead tree, and the only thing worse than that is watching a tree die. I have heard that when it is cold and foggy and it rains, more men hang themselves. If you are outside in such weather that news might not depress you. How sad that this should not be depressing. But the saddest thing of all is a dead or dying tree in the rain and snow, its bark shiny with death, glistening in a gray slick, leaves long left. A great hollow melancholy settles over such a tree, a fog of gloom. If near, you are enveloped in this gloom, this ghastly fit of depression. But worse than that is when several such trees are clumped together, a graveyard of gray trunks, all pumped up and hollow, sick and lifeless, absolutely sucked out. Imagine now a forest of these trees. Imagine now the ground all ashes and grit, not fit to grow. Imagine the air yellow and poisonous, packed with sulfur and other pestilent gases. Imagine the sun a yellow mist, trying to break through this muck, failing, the light faint, a glimmer, becoming leaden. Suppose now that it will remain like this. Suppose

Hammer. Nail. Wood.

there is no hope. Suppose. What would you do if given a
branch, a rope?

    And what are you doing now to reduce the carbon dioxide
from being pumped into the air?

The music is lovely when they play it right.

THE JUNKYARD OWNER. The lumberyard dealer. The sound of steel, the rhythm of lumber, the melody of economics. Used metal is purchased by the pound. Usually. Lumber is purchased by the running foot, the board foot, the panel (4-by-8, or whatever), the strip, or the hurricane. The last is a familiar and convenient (to the lumber dealer) unit. Example: After the hurricane in Florida where all those homes were demolished, the price of a standard sheet of plywood went up by 33% to 150%. No offense, please, this is business. If you had bid on a job that had plywood in it before the hurricane and you didn't include a hurricane fudge factor, you lose. Consider yourself lucky, after the hurricane, to even be getting plywood at those advanced prices, and don't say a word about the quality of the plywood you're getting. Just nail it on. Pound away.

Emile had all those PCBs from the Niagara Mohawk transformers that soaked into the soil on his farm. Skyler had them too. No one told Emile about PCBs, nor did they tell Skyler. This is cheap farming country up here, about as cheap as you can get, and if you have a little money and employ a few people you can get away with a lot. The Niagara Mohawk man who came out to hook up my electricity spent twenty minutes complaining about all the subsidized energy-saving devices that big institutions were installing. All the while he kept the engine on his truck running. Wouldn't even shut it off. I guess that was his way of getting back at us. Eventually, Skyler started to worry about PCBs. Even Emile. After Emile's wife saw the devil chasing the school bus she baked some angel food cakes for the PTA. She wouldn't use Proctor & Gamble because they used the devil sign on their logo. I don't know what she used, Arrowhead Mills maybe. After she got there and set her cakes up on the folding table in the church basement and sat down to pour Murine in her eyes and light up a Lucky she saw some chocolate cakes next to hers and thought they were devil's food cakes and made to knock them off the table into the funeral urn but Skyler's wife had baked those cakes and she was steamed about her cakes getting shoved around. That was a fuss. Emile and Skyler were both there. They paid no mind. Later in the evening Skyler started to change colors and began to choke. They took him to the hospital in Ogdensburg but he died on a side street before they could unload him. His wife was there. She had her finger on his wrist the whole way in and she could feel the erratic throb that went through his veins and she could feel it in the alley until she couldn't feel it anymore, when it just stopped. She had brought one of her devil's food cakes with her to give to the ambulance drivers, sort of a thank you, and even Emile's wife had come and brought one of her cakes, too, though she wasn't in the ambulance. The river is right there, the St. Lawrence, a wide busy river, crammed with boats and the parts from boats that Skyler and Emile would buy from and sell to.

Sun, wind, rain, clouds, sunsets, rain.

W HEN YOU BUILD you pay attention to the weather. Heat, humidity, cold, rain, freezing. They all affect your building. Even the sun does. The sun gives warmth and ease to building, gives its blessing to building. You can build in rain but it is no fun, not that building needs to be fun. A measure of fun, of joy, makes the building go easier. Rain is good for curing concrete, so the ideal situation would be sun while you set up the forms and pour concrete and then after it sets, after several hours, a gentle rain, all through the night and for the next several days, then cloudy, humid, cloudy, rain again, humid, cloudy. Let the concrete dry slowly, cure, so it will set up strong. After a week or so of soft rain, let the sun slowly come out, the concrete slowly dry out. Now, no more rain for several weeks, several months, or rain only at night. No freezing. Tell the weather not to freeze. If you are building in the fall, as we were, you must explain this to the weather. Be gentle but firm. This is important. Up here near the St. Lawrence River it will freeze at night in the fall, but it is not something you especially want, certainly you do not want it when the concrete is curing or when you are moving the earth, digging, putting in drainage, a septic system. No freeze.

After Skyler left, Harlow sort of pined for him. No one would explain to him how he could have lived after he had been thrown out of that Plymouth and skidded down the road, how he had in fact, hardly been hurt. Skyler was the only one who would explain that to him and Skyler didn't even explain it to him, he just listened and Harlow thought he was explaining it. He wasn't. Skyler was as dumbfounded as Harlow. Harlow thought there was some mystery involved, something about American Indians or aliens. It had nothing to do with God. He did not live the kind of life that God would interfere with. In general it was a rather degrading life he led and he knew that God had little to do with people like him.

Calling on friends for an act of kindness.

I, REALLY WE, MY WIFE AND I, have asked them to drive eight hours from a large eastern city into this northern wilderness, this cold dairy country just below the St. Lawrence River, and to bring their hammers and warm clothes, waterproof clothes, and to spend a weekend nailing plywood and framing in some studding, and offered in return the possibility of camping in the meadow just in time to appreciate the freezing fall and to celebrate the return of frigid weather. Dick, Chris, Antek, Rick, two Carols, two Marys, two Franks, Bob, Sybil, Marcia, Dea, Masca, Corum, Ashen, three-year-old Claire, sons of one of the Marys—Brian and Eamon—Patricia, Brendan, Siobhan, my wife Patricia's parents Edith and Frank. Roast chicken and pretzels from Pennsylvania, the rest of the food from here. The overpriced plywood is put up by the underpriced help. We celebrate that night with a party and just to make sure we haven't forgotten do the same thing the next night. I am reminded that it really is not my house, not even our house, but it is the house of all who have helped, all who have been here, and that I am lucky. I give thanks.

The ruin of a
perfectly good junkyard.

Skyler enhanced his old farm. He had
bought it years ago when it was something organic, a green
and smelly mixture of manure and seed, oats, hay, crops.
Trees curved down into the meadows with little effort. Water,
green and stagnant, lay in syrupy pools about the farm. Fences
had fallen and brush had grown up. The old green thrust, the
fuss of vegetation, the flutter of cicadas in the summer pre-
sented an idyllic picture of a neglected farm: old, rambling,
worn, weary, and lush. He changed that. In a grassy meadow
with a pond he had piled his cars and his transmissions and
axle housings and PCB-bleeding electric transformers from
Niagara Mohawk, arranged them in neat rows like a crop of
machinery. The crankcase oil seeped into the pond and it
seemed to revive it, producing huge, flagrant aquatic plants
and vicious blood-red worms. The PCBs dripped into soil
that was later shipped down to North Carolina where they
like that kind of thing.

When Skyler died his widow sold the junkyard but not the
land. The rusting cars and devilish transformers were taken
away and in place of that beloved muck and oil, that slick,

greasy metallic residue we walked through to claim what we needed, grass (grass!) began to appear like some mutant growth. Tiny droppings from the birds, manure, soil, produced an avalanche of green, yellow and red, even blue. But nothing renews the heart like a piece of rusting machinery set in a grassy meadow. She was not able to remove all the machinery, all the axle housings, all the loops of cable. The meadows had been reclaimed as meadows, but some cars refused to be moved and took root like weeds in the hummocky soil, resting and rusting in the slow dignity of time. There was a chicken coop that stored perpetual motion springs. Someone had convinced Skyler that he could build a perpetual motion machine and make millions if he could find the right spring, and he collected hundreds, thousands of them and stored them in an old chicken coop with broken windows and a tin roof and wrapped them in black plastic. Just before he died he told Harlow about his scheme but this only puzzled Harlow, who was still fixed on his own situation. He couldn't see what perpetual motion springs had to do with that. He asked Skyler about the connection and Skyler told him to forget about his accident. It is unimportant, Skyler said.

And then they were gone.

FRIENDS DRIVE BACK TO THE CITY and we are left with our building, a post-and-beam structure twenty by thirty feet, almost thirty feet tall. Coming down the road you can see the tall, sharply peaked roof and the less steep porch roof and it looks like a toy house. The dimensions, though slightly tall, seem too perfect for a real house. What seems strange is that after several months of work, after the foundation has been laid and the deck built and the timbers put up and the roof rafters secured and the roof put on and the walls studded and plywood put up to secure the building for the winter, it suddenly seems as if there is more work to do than when the building was just an idea. Suddenly, details flood in where they hadn't existed before, where only the structure existed. Before we built, it seemed simple, straightforward. Suddenly it has become vastly complicated. Second-floor joists, bathroom, stairway, wiring, plumbing, sewer to hook up to the septic field, heating, studding for interior walls, insulation, windows, skylights; all the details I had deliberately ignored before, and so had forgotten about, come to the fore. And money. Uh oh. We've been much too casual about

120

money. It's already cost us thousands more than we expected, mainly because our expectations were so unrealistic. We've spent all our money to get to where we are, we've spent more than our money in fact. But where will the money come from to move on from here? And we must move on. Putting up a building is giving birth. You can't stop it even if you wanted to. A building has its own life and will not be denied. A building screams for its own "itness." You dare not prevent it from being. Moreover, I think of all the mistakes I've made. We never had any plans for an architect to look at, much less have an architect draw up plans. We never had the soil tested. Never had experts advise us about site or weather or anything else. We simply walked on the land and where the land felt good—said, here—here is where we put our building. It seems a very unscientific way to build a house. The only instruments we used were compass and tape measure. Imagine spending thousands of dollars and starting with a compass and a tape measure. Oh folly, oh fools. We could not afford a cellar and so simply put in a crawl space. Perhaps it is not deep enough. We did not put the drainage tile all the way around the house, only on the uphill side where the water might collect. That too was probably a mistake. It should have gone all the way around. The timbers are big but I am not sure about the bracing. I have no knee braces, those triangulated braces for the joints. I must put them in. What if a huge high wind comes? What if the *feng sui* is not right? Taxes will go up. Can we afford them? Insurance? Roof rafters that are not the proper dimension? But oh, I love this house. I really do.

Harlow got married but it did him little good. He was hardly married. She was a small evil-looking woman though she was far from evil, was in fact a good woman. She took Harlow's child and raised him in her belly and when he was born she

121

up and left, or Harlow left her and moved into another trailer and she asked for child support and he wouldn't give it so she had him jailed and that didn't help either. Harlow didn't seem to care much about his kid. Harlow didn't think that was normal but the normal hardly bothered him. He had only a nodding acquaintance with it. When the weather was good he liked to take apart a Kawasaki motorcycle engine and leave the parts spread out on his front yard. He would arrange the parts in the kind of formation the Chinese used when they busted down from the hills in Korea and when the rain came Harlow would run back into his trailer and watch the Kawasaki motorcycle engine parts get rained on. He bought that motorcycle from Skyler and when he bought it, it ran, but once he took it apart it never ran again. Harlow had the only trailer I've ever seen that rusted. I didn't know they could do that. Someone asked Harlow's wife why she left him and she said, "He never talks. All he wants to do is look at my bottom." She wanted to give someone else that chance so she married elsewhere, downstate, somewhere near Syracuse. Harlow went down once and scared her new man and that seemed to satisfy him and he never went down there again.

He took Skyler's passing hard. We all did. There was something about Skyler that made you think he was a hero. Skyler was one of those men you just like to be around. He had this ease about him, this enthusiasm, as if he was always looking for something and he didn't mind if you came along with him. It wasn't just the perpetual springs, it was something else. And Harlow had that need in him to be looking for something, as if by stabbing the Chinese he had put a hole in himself. I think Harlow was tired of watching people die, but then again it may have been something else.

Stuff.

MEN IN THE NORTH spend a lot of their time collecting stuff. They buy whatever stuff they can get and build a garage where they can nail their stuff to the wall and when it gets really cold they turn the heater on and open the garage door so everyone who drives buy can see all the stuff they have in their garage. Quite a bit, usually. If you don't have much stuff you're not much of a man in the north. Not at all. If the guy next door to you, a couple of hundred yards down the road or several miles away in the next town, has more stuff you better do something about that.

You can buy stuff anywhere. Men came out to Skyler's when he was alive and to Emile's to buy stuff. Skyler never liked to sell stuff. He would always ask them, "Where's the dream in that?" Emile, it was OK by him. He made money selling stuff and he also made money trucking it. He sold stuff but you had to get it out of there yourself, all by yourself. If you needed help Emile would charge you extra and he'd charge extra too for delivery. He liked that. It was a good way to make money, especially on heavy stuff he had a hard time selling. It was like selling the same stuff twice, three times.

Hammer. Nail. Wood.

Emile would sell you stuff by the pound and then he would hit you with a chain tax, depending upon how many chains he had to wrap around your purchase. Harlow helped him sometimes. But Harlow's strong point was not customer relations and if you said something about the way the chains were wrapped around the stuff Harlow would dump it on your lawn and come back without the money and when Emile asked him about the money he'd tell him to get it himself.

A fight in a bar. Two guys were arguing about their stuff. They were big and fat and too lazy to get off their bar stools so they kept punching each other sitting down, knocking over glasses and beers and bleeding. The bartender kept coming over and telling them to stop but he was hooted down and they just kept punching each other. Smack! Bam! All about stuff. Finally Harlow came over and knocked them both off their bar stools. Everyone thought they'd get up and punch and we'd get to see some real punching. But they kept lying on the floor, punching, punching little piddling punches because they were lying down. "Get up," someone shouted. "Get up you ratfuck assholes! Punch like a man!" But they couldn't get up so guys held each one up so they could keep on hitting. They kept sliding down and everyone was upset. How could they be so lazy? Then someone noticed that they both had broken legs. That was from the last time they had argued about their stuff.

Put your fist through it and see if it's still standing.

I DON'T WANT TO HURT ANYTHING that can walk, Harlow said. I don't want to punch anything that can fly or swim or crawl or anything that makes a motion of itself, that moves of itself, that has the energy in itself. That left all the things that just stood around, that didn't move. I don't want to hurt anything that can grow, that can change, anything that's green or has the color of life to it. Nothing that sighs when it breaks. Nothing that moans. That left a lot of other things. Or if there is some kind of thing that we don't know about that will do these things, some unknown thing, that I don't want to hurt. That deserves peace. Don't you think so? That left a lot of doors and windows and walls, shower curtains, chairs, machines with phosphorescent screens.

The small, the substantial, the silly.

W<small>INTER IS COMING</small> and we are leaving this home. It must weather the roaring, rattling winds and the snow loads without us. Squirrel nests, hornet hives, skunk dens may find their way in but I hope not. I hope the mice do not nibble at the walls or the wiring, and that they leave the bulbs alone, and that bears do not use the house as a huge scratching board. Plastic must be placed where the plywood joins at top and bottom so the rain and snow do not get in and ruin the plywood. The earth around the house must be put where it belongs before it's frozen. Openings must be sealed up. The building site must be cleaned, lumber put away, tools stored, nails picked up or nailed in boards that need them. Pulleys removed from roof rafters. Ladders taken in from the outside of the house. A pitless adapter for the well. A window guard for the window in the crawl space. A nailer for the porch rafters, which means more studs in the wall. Flashing for the porch roof, which means cutting the tin for the flashing, which means finding an electric outlet for the circular saw because cutting tin with a snips or a hand saw is a hellish job, which I end up doing anyway. This is just the beginning.

Putting a building to bed, getting it ready for its hibernation is a series in a long list of things that need to be done, that can't be put off. A stunning realization that you must leave it here half-built until spring, until you can come up and spend months, more months, years, making it ready.

Harlow blew up his trailer and didn't have much of a place to stay. He moved into the old railroad station that had been bought by a deranged Amish man and moved to the Amish man's farm now that the passenger trains don't run through the Junction anymore. The Amish man had the railroad station set up on concrete blocks. It was a huge piece of wood, this station, tons and tons of it, about thirty feet high and sixty feet long, gray and blue. At one time when there were jobs in factories here people had come and gone from that station, moving down or moving up. The station was a great starting-off point, the official place that signaled people's lives were changing. It made people proud to go to that station and it made them proud to meet someone at that station and the people who built it and designed it knew that and made the station accordingly. There was the right balance of heavy timbers and light decoration, the flimsy and the substantial, wood and glass, steel and stone. The floor was marble. The Amish man didn't take that with him. You can still see that marble floor by the railroad tracks, underneath mud and manure and weeds. The marble had a brass line built into it. When Harlow was a boy he would go to the railroad station and pull his wooden train on that brass line, making sure one of the wheels rode over the brass. He was disappointed that the Amish man hadn't brought the marble and he offered to go over and get the marble for him and carry it back, slab by slab, which he would have to break up in smaller pieces, although evidently in those days they had had the muscle to handle those big slabs. There was a good argument for putting the slabs in the station. It was tall to begin with, made taller by sitting on concrete blocks and then plopped on the side of a hill. If a good wind came tumbling down the hill it could topple the station. Maybe the marble would anchor it. But the Amish man said no. He didn't think it made much difference to the hay or sheep, and that was what, who, Harlow was sharing the railroad station with. Harlow liked the station. Most of the windows were covered with hay, the insides were filled with hay, and as soon as Harlow took up occupancy the Amish man kicked the sheep out. That left Harlow and the hay. There are worse things to share a railroad station with. The station was on the side of a shallow hill with a gentle rise, and overlooked a county road. There was a girl Harlow brought there. She wasn't too quick but she knew how to do bees. She was the only person he knew who could pet bees. A fat bee would crawl on her index finger and then she would take the other finger and stroke it on the head, under the head, on the wings. "You could do it," she said, "just be careful not to get stung." In the fall she would go out and gather the honey no one else could and she lived in an old barn where she kept honeycombs. Bees would do for her what they wouldn't for others, not that she didn't get stung. She did. She was tall and rangy with brown stringy hair that she never washed. She never wore dresses. Boots, shorts, a Carhart jacket, summer and winter. Then the Amish man told Harlow she had to leave. Between her and the railroad station Harlow chose. She went back to the barn. Harlow went to the barn often to look at her legs. She had long legs with brown bumps and scars from the bees. There was a white salve, a lanolin, she rubbed on her legs to keep them smooth from the scratches and Harlow liked to watch her put the salve on because every time she did it she licked her finger before dipping it into the jar and scooping out a fingerful to rub on her calves. "It almost makes me forget the Chinese," he told Emile. He also said this to Emile: "It doesn't take very much." No one knew what he meant. They lay in the fields at night and tried to count the number of stars that moved. Then one day she stabbed him in the thigh. She refused to see him after that.

Sitting, watching, waiting.

IT WAS A CURIOUS THING to do. For months he sat on the ridge next to a grove of sugar maples and watched us work. He never said a word, at least not to us. Most of his talking was done to Skyler and when Skyler left I don't know who he talked to. He lived on disability. One cold, windy, wet fall day when the leaves were yapping at the wind and the ground was losing its green, I made my way over to Emile's for a ring nut. Emile's place was situated on a high hill and the junkyard part yawned down on you from the hill. You needed some good machinery to get up the road and if you didn't know any better you might think it was just a messy farmer who lived here, someone who never threw anything away. But as soon as you started up the pot-holed driveway, that boulder-infested stretch of gravel and earth clogged with miniature swimming pools, you began to realize that no sane man could possibly collect in his front yard what Emile had in his. Refrigerator warehouses of twenty and thirty years ago had been emptied out and dumped near the top of the hill and the fridges tumbled down, caught at various points on the hillside. White trucks, Ferguson tractors, New Holland combines were exploded over the hill. Tractor tires leaned against a punctured silo. A barn was full of rusty linotype machines, cream separators and jigs for extruded aluminum storm doors and windows. Rolls of rusted screen, wooden boxes full of water and washers still wrapped in greasy butcher paper, milking stools, radiators, hose, thresher parts, bolts of indeterminate vintage, gray barn beams, bales of hay, broken toilets, cracked sinks, castings, cores of copper windings, cattle troughs. I yelled for Emile and realized he would never hear me. There was too much junk around for the shouts to get trapped in. Several smaller barns and buildings were scattered about the house, bursting with metal and grease, oxen yokes, anvils, aluminum pans, windows stacked and broken, broken with glee and collected by Emile in his silent, stiff way and stacked next to a wall that several months later would slowly give way, spilling its rich innards into the yard, and when winter came the snow blew through the hole and piled itself higher and higher inside the small barn, like some pussy boil that got bigger and bigger and refused to burst. I made my way to the house, which looked like several smaller houses stacked together and then compressed, walls pushing through walls and doors slanted, askew. From the porch windows I could see them in the kitchen but there was no stairway up to the porch nor was there a door onto the porch. I walked around the back, through an opening where a door used to be, into a woodshed that held no wood but was darkened with old metal objects, dull and blunted, greasy and knobbed, a dirt floor, and saw another door that was almost the kitchen door but wasn't, a door to a room next to the kitchen, this room with a real floor, a wood floor anyway, and another door at the end. This room had old grocery carts and anchor line, foil TV-dinner trays, bones, dog food, maple syrup cans, and several burst bags of cement, which had partially hardened and held the cans to the carts. I walked up to the door and opened it. A bright glare. Heat. This was the kitchen. A long table, slanted, linoleum in various shades, grades, and levels on the floor. Too many things in the room to mention but a TV at one corner of the room, ignored by everyone. A weatherman was trying to explain what was happening to the weather. Emile sat at one corner of the table in a T-shirt. His face was a topographic tumble, metamorphic rock with dark schist and an outwash of gullies and valleys, planes, lines, bumps. Em was standing at the other end of the kitchen, talking to no one in particular, talking to no one in fact, with immense joy. Emile was listening to Paul who had come for a pushrod for the Continental engine. Harlow was in one corner of the room. He and Emile were silent. It was the first time I had ever been inside a room with Harlow. The great heat of the room seemed to have shaken the dirt off everything and dropped it to the floor where it hardened and brightened. The floor glistened and shone in a gritty way. The heat in the room was unbearable. I hoped I would not have to stay long in the room. Paul smiled when I came in. Emile was unable to smile. We all understood that. There was a baseball bat in the corner. Harlow had his eye on that. He looked like he wanted to grab it and run.

Do you really need a second floor?

THIS BIG TINKERTOY IS UP. The tin roof is on (nailed in a windstorm). The plywood panels are nailed to the outside. The well is dug. Septic tank and septic field dug and buried. The porch is built, though one of the porch beams, a twenty-foot 8-by-10, fell about ten feet off the shovel of the backhoe onto the porch with a sickening thud, sounding like a sack of one hundred watermelons dropped on a dance floor. Gray clay is piled around the house. It reaches up to grab at your feet when you step, and sludges up on your shoes. You walk in mud even after you've left the mud. From the road the house looks like I imagined it would look: a tall toy house. The red tin roof sparkles dully in the sun and I can imagine the crescendo it makes in rain. It is an orchestra for rain.

Inside, wood timbers hold the house in huge fingers, and 2-by-6s are studded between them to provide a base for the plywood sheathing. The space rises up and up, twelve feet, sixteen, eighteen, twenty-three feet at the center. A huge wooded space. Each of the woods has its own smell, from the sharp vomit-like smell of hemlock to the spice of pine.

A second floor? Why cut off that beautiful space? Why not leave it open, soaring? Let your eye be captured by the magnificence of rising wood. Let the soaring timbers breathe.

But we decide to put in a second floor. Cathedral ceilings look good in picture books about rustic country homes that cost hundreds of thousands of dollars but they are wasteful and expensive. If you really want the right look in a cathedral ceiling it must be wood, and that means you must build another ceiling above the wood to provide the insulation you need. In winter, most of your heat is going to drift up to the top of that ceiling and stay there while you shiver below, unless you really pile on the heat. Finally, you're losing a lot of potential bedroom space. Of course if you're a successful artist, or even a not-too-successful doctor or lawyer, you can afford to build a bigger house and put your bedrooms on the ground floor. But if you're like me, you can't afford a bigger house. You've got to get the most out of the one you have. The bedrooms go in. That way we can also take advantage of the heat that drifts up. Stick in a few skylights and in the summer the air will dance through the house. Plus, room for guests, like my daughter Julie, her husband Andy, and their daughter Natalie.

This house reminds me why tools look better than kitchen appliances. They are all function. They are designed to let the hand fit better on the tool or the tool work better in the wood. Here too, all the wood has a reason. It is holding up walls and floors. It is providing a frame for something to be nailed to. It offers channels for insulation.

It is a clunky space, this house. It's like Goofy. Ah-yup!

Harlow wondered why no one had ever seen God up here. Em had seen the devil but no one had ever seen the Virgin Mary rising out of a pile of dirty bedsheets or the face of sweet Jesus in a torn billboard poster. Maybe that was why the Amish had been sent up here. They had been sent up here to recruit Him. But if He wouldn't come for the Amish, who would He come for?

Indian ghosts, exotic lands.

NEW YORK IS UNGLAMOROUS when it comes to myth. Real meaning lies elsewhere. We travel to reach the "authentic" lands, the arboreal forests of the Northwest, the glazed canyons of Utah and New Mexico, the pink Pacific sunsets, the songlines and petroglyphs of Australia, the lush jungles and *fer-de-lance* danger of Brazil, the icy beauty of Norway and Finland. Aborigines, Pygmies, Celts, Franks, Greeks, Zulus, Serbs, Saxons, and Kurds are honored for their homeland and their ancient ways, songs, stories, meanings, and myths. Shamans and Medicine Men, Priests and Chiefs are revered, as long as they are from somewhere out west. Cheyennes, Apache, Lakota Sioux, Crow, Hopi, Navajo, all seem more romantic, more "Indian," more Native American than the Confederacy of the Iroquois: the Seneca, the Mohawk, the Onondaga, the Oneida, the Cayuga, and later the Tuscaroras. The latter are almost cartoon Indians, caricatures of Native Americans (having the misfortune to have as their popular historian James Fenimore Cooper).

What a shame. The Iroquois are, as the great ethnologist John Collier recognized, the most important Indian grouping on the continent, north of Mexico. "I think no institutional achievement of mankind exceeds it (the Confederacy of the Iroquois) in either wisdom or intelligence—accepting the limits of its time and place." Like many great nations they were both horrible and honorable. They were not passive, they were not polite. Their contribution to Western civilization is amazing. Astounding would be a better word. Somehow, it has been kept a secret. Somehow, we have come to believe that our constitution sprang full blown from the genius of a few enlightened but transplanted Europeans. It did not. It was heavily borrowed from the Iroquois with, of course, no credit. And the seat of their great power was close to the St. Lawrence River, in Canada and New York State. The land that we built on is land that was once under the tutelage of the Iroquois Confederacy. Spiritually, it still is.

What it comes down to is that Emile must put boxed channel-steel bars on the sides of his truck so engine blocks do not fall off. The county legislature passed a law because a tourist in a Winnebago, though no one could imagine what a tourist would be doing here since there is nothing that calls for tourists or tourism, had to dodge a falling Toyota engine block and ran off the road, smashing an Amish potato stand. Emile found out that the only God-given right he had was to pay a fine and get his truck impounded, or put on sides. He complained to Harlow and Harlow told him that he would take care of it, but Paul's father finally talked sense into the both of them. Then again, maybe it wasn't sense he talked into them but something else. Whatever it was, it worked. That was the second time I was in Emile's kitchen. Em was talking to the weatherman on the TV though she didn't really expect him to talk back and Emile was sitting at the table in a T-shirt looking as dirty as any man I have ever seen. He had just finished talking to Harlow and Harlow had made his famous pronouncement about authority and looked around for Emile's baseball bat when Paul's father said, "Wait, just wait." At least that's what I think he said, though he may have said more. But what he did then, what he did next . . . so strange. He reached over and touched Harlow. Just touched him on the arm, the forearm. I don't think Harlow had been touched in a long time. That was all he did. Just touch him. And Harlow, he just settled down, he didn't look for the bat. Paul's father didn't say anything after that. No one did. Even Em turned around. I felt embarrassed. It was one of those moments where something incredibly important has taken place and you don't quite know what it is but you do know that everyone else in the room knows exactly what it is. Exactly. Even Emile seems to know, and he comes as close to smiling as I've ever seen any man. I wanted to say, "What was that all about?" I didn't, of course. It would have spoiled something.

The Home Comfort cook stove.

ABOUT FIFTEEN YEARS AGO land was cheap in St. Lawrence County; dairy farms were going out of business. At the same time a group of Amish in Ohio were being crowded out by population and land prices and began looking for somewhere else to settle. Two problems became one solution. The Amish began moving here. Farms were bought and Amish families and a church bishop moved up from Ohio. The locals offered hostility and acceptance. Amish sawmills, cider presses, fruit and produce stands, maple syrup, quilts, eggs, milk, butter. Amish tables, chairs, porch swings. Amish carpenter/contractors (who could and did underbid the locals). Amish chimney builders, buggy makers and repairers, blacksmiths appeared; there were a host of new and old skills and services, products, and markets. The Amish bishop lived on the next farm, and the school was on his farm, and every morning, Amish time, we heard the sound of horse hooves and over the rise came a black buggy racing down the hill. Inside the buggy were two of the prettiest young girls you've ever seen—Amish schoolteachers—laughing and chattering to themselves and when they saw us on the roof they waved and we waved back and they laughed and hid their faces and raced on to the school. In the afternoon they came back up the road, still laughing and talking, the horse slowing because he was going uphill, and they always turned and waved, and smiled, a little subdued from their work at school, and we always stopped whatever it was we were doing and watched the horse pull that buggy up the hill and thought about those beautiful girls with their dark hair and dark clothes, and wondered why they weren't married yet, wondered who would marry them, wondered about all the children they would have. We always kept our eyes on them, until the buggy crested the top of the hill, partially hidden by the immature elms that lined the road and the shower of leaves that stirred behind the buggy wheels, and finally dropped out of view. We never tired of watching them and they, apparently, never tired of waving to us. It was a moment in the day when I felt remarkably calm, remarkably lucky.

It was the same way I felt going into Isaac Hostetler's home. He was an Amish man who lived a mile from us. He made tents, tarpaulins, and awnings, kept chickens and goats, and had a small sawmill. We had an old Home Comfort cook stove, a wood stove, that sat out in the field a hundred feet or so from the building site. It was covered with a heavy plastic tarp, weighted down with scrap lumber. It was cast iron and white porcelain and had an iron fire box that supplied heat to the entire stove, the flames rushing under the stove top lids and circling around a water box and then up and around a flue, which curled around a bread warmer. The stove top lids could be taken off, ring by ring, and a pot or pan placed on, adjacent to the slanted flames, which rushed by in a roar as they headed for the flue, and not only heated the room well but cooked even better. Made in the forties, it was neither modern nor old-fashioned and needed attention. It drooped, sagged, had pieces bent or worn. The lid-holder notches of the stove-top lids had lost their edge so it was difficult to pick them up. We left the stove in the field until we decided what to do with it. Too big, too cumbersome for the house we were building. We had given an old Navy mess tent that had been given to us for the work weekend to Isaac, and when he came to collect it he saw the stove sitting in the field. The Amish do not waste, and they recognize value. He asked if the stove was for sale. I decided on the spot that it was. My wife agreed. He bent to his knees and slowly began opening the doors to the stove, picking up the stove lids, turning the crank on the fire box that settled the ashes into a pan below, examined the flue, inspected the water box, looked for what needed to be fitted, what needed to be adjusted, rebent, reshaped, and then stood up when he was finished. The whole process took about fifteen minutes, longer. He was not about to be rushed. "What might you be asking for it?" he said. I named a price $15 less than what I thought I could get for it. He rubbed his chin. "I'll have to talk to my wife," he said, "but probably, probably, we will. I'll have to talk to my wife." The next day two of his girls came by in a buggy and dropped the money off in an envelope with a note he wrote on paper from Stauffer's Harness Shop in Mt. Pleasant Mills. The next day we loaded the stove on the bed of the pickup truck and drove it to his farm. His wife answered the door. She looked too young to have as many children as she did. The inside of the house was dark and clean. The floors were polished wood, wide and uneven. The walls were light gray and the wood borders at the top and the bottom and the frame running around the door and the board that bisected the wall and ran around the room was dark blue, light gray framed in dark blue. There were several kerosene lanterns on the table, along with fifty loaves of bread in plastic wrappers for market. A girl of eight held a child of four. An eleven-year-old was working at a sewing machine making quilts. A child of fifteen months was crawling on the floor, and stopped to look up. The mother held a four-month-old. There were other children scampering on the stairs. The older boys were outside working in the silo. In the dark room the children's faces reminded me of faces painted by the Italian Renaissance painters: Fra Filippo Lippi, Caravaggio, and Tintoretto. They were full of light and intensity. An unblemished wonder shown through, sparked by amazement and curiosity. What was the source of light that blazed from those young faces?

Emile seems pained when he drives down the road. The manic has gone out of his eyes. His engine blocks are now safely tucked away on the bed of his truck, not just hemmed in by steel-bar sides but chained down and ratcheted tight with quick clamps. He no longer has Skyler to argue with and bid against for a wreck on Rt. 11 or when Niagara Mohawk wants to get rid of more transformers. He's worried that junkyards are going out of fashion, not that they were ever really fashionable, but there was always a certain amount of trade he could depend on. Folks, mainly farmers, reused "stuff" and that meant if he had a piece of iron lying around in his yard that used to do something, lift something, or propel something, or gear up or gear down, or separate something, or sift it or slice it or chop it, or throw it up in the air for who knows what reason, there was always somebody he could count on to come by and say yes! I want that there, I want to make it rechop, reslice, re-move, I want to get this whole contraption moving again, get the gears oiled and new wheels on and new pulleys on and get this darn thing working again and it's only going to cost me a fraction of what it would new. That's right! Just a fraction. Now they wanted to melt everything down and start new. They wanted to bury it. They wanted to "re-cycle" it, which meant not fixing it up but crushing it or melt-ing it or completely disintegrating it into something new. The Amish were his salvation. They knew how to reuse, refix. They knew all about salvation. Emile would have Isaac over and they'd sit talking at the kitchen table and Emile would sell him something cheap that he could use and then they'd talk some and Emile would throw in something else and they'd talk longer and Emile would throw in more, and Isaac would get embarrassed at all the stuff Emile was tossing his way, giving him, and when he tried to pay him back, with maple syrup or tent awnings or cider, Emile would insist on giving him more, accepting a few dollars for it. It was a Potlach, except that Emile didn't call it that and didn't consciously set out to try and outgive anyone, not that there was anyone to outgive. Isaac then would get stuck with all this stuff. Most of it he could use, he could fix. That was the problem. He couldn't just take it. It wasn't fair. You had to be fair about things. Pay a fair price for things. Work for a fair wage. Not cheat anyone. Not take advantage. And here Emile was doing all this for him. It wasn't fair. He liked Emile but he avoided going to see Emile and then Emile got upset and thought he was snubbing him and then Emile thought maybe there was a reason Isaac was snubbing him, that Emile wasn't leading a Godly enough life, was too much of a degenerate. OK, Emile would admit to that. Sure. After all, he ran a junkyard. Wasn't that kind of de-generate? But the funny thing of it was that Isaac had never said anything to him, had never proselytized or suggested they get down on their knees in the kitchen or even men-tioned God. Never did any of that. Never sounded pious or holy either. Just regular. He liked that about Isaac. He liked Isaac because Isaac never lied and never bragged and did ex-actly what he said he was going to do and Emile thought, damn! That's not a bad way to be. Damn! Isaac even seemed to like him, never held it against him that he ran a junkyard the way some others did. So Emile was doubly puzzled by the way Isaac was acting. Doubly puzzled. He'd go over to Isaac's farm and Isaac's wife would say that Isaac was out in the field or over to Gouverneur selling potatoes or somesuch. He'd sit in his kitchen on Wednesday afternoon waiting for Isaac to come by, and he never did. Never did. Well, you never knew about people. You never knew. Paul's father came by and Harlow and they sat and talked, mostly about machinery. And Emile. For the first time he felt sad. Junk wasn't making much money for him. His wife, Em, had got a job stuffing envelopes at home and they figured once she was making 67¢ an hour doing that and then she got a job in a sheet-metal factory, putting the crimps on air-conditioning ducts, and she was lucky to get that, real lucky. She made minimum wage, around two and a half dollars an hour, minus the kickbacks of course, and so they made out. Emile had convinced her that the devil hated sheet metal, that you could never find Beelzebub around it, and she accepted that. Now she got to saying "Well that's a blessing" after everything you told her, everything she said, everything she noticed, except of course for those things that were not blessings. But once she said to one of her fellow workers on the line, a three-hundred-pound French Canadian lady who lived in a trailer with seven children whose husband made road calls for the U-haul rental, "Sometimes I wonder what this life is about." She was working on some heating ducts for a new bank that had just opened, a big banking chain that had bought up several local banks and was instituting new loan policies. Winter was coming and business would get slow. She would be laid off and people didn't buy much junk in the winter. Emile's yard would be covered with snow, often not lifting until spring, and then the junkyard would only exist in Emile's mind. He would remember where all the cream separators were located, which snow pile held the axle springs and which pile held the crimped radiators. Water, rust, he didn't mind that in his junkyard. Hell! That's what it was all about. No one would buy anything from him if it wasn't rusty. They were getting more than they paid for, some iron oxide thrown in, extra, free. Winter was tough. You sold less in winter. Folks were usually laid off at the beginning of winter and then hired back in the spring and you had to find a way to make it through the cold months. Animals and people, the same. The more social-istic counties in the state, those in the south and in the big cities, they had services for people you could get to, but up here in St. Lawrence County it was different. How could you apply for welfare if you didn't even have the gas or a car to drive the twenty or thirty miles it took to go to the social ser-vice agency? They made you come back anyway because they really didn't even want you in the first place and let you know that, right away, let you know that you were some kind of sludge, some sewer grub for daring to apply for welfare. Not that most folks did. Most of them would rather starve. Pride did not go before a fall here. People fell. But somehow Emile made it through each winter. He and Em held on close and tight, hugging each other in bed, his big bony arms wrapping themselves around her tight, tiny body, several times around it seemed. They were not a handsome pair, truth be told, but they got by. Love. Yes. Love. Paul's father had most of his teeth missing because he couldn't afford new teeth and the few that he had left were in the front of his mouth and held his ciga-rette in place but he could still talk a blue streak and knew how to smile, and like his son, if it was machinery and it ran once, he could get it running again. His hands had talc grained in, could never wash it out, and if the mine hadn't closed down he wouldn't have been able to work much longer anyway because of the stiffness the talc made and there was nothing about that in the union contract, the UMW contract, not that the mine felt obliged to follow that contract too closely, no sir, not when profits got low. But don't talk to Paul's father about that. You'd be a whiner and a complainer if you did, and he hates whiners. "People got to be responsible for themselves. It's a free country. Man pays you good money to work. What you belly-aching for?" You could hardly argue with that. And did I mention that Emile and Em, E & E, had a Home Comfort cook stove?

The man who loved Amish.

FRED IS RICH, rich for up north. He likes to hang around the Amish. He has no children, no wife, no family. Put him in the city and he wouldn't be that rich, just well off. But up here he's rich and he can do just about anything he wants. What he wants is to hang around Amish. He has a lot of Amish friends and he likes nothing better than to be in the middle of an Amish maelstrom, children racing back and forth pushing scooters or wagons or running for an old tire hung from a tree. The Amish do not mind him. If that is what he wants that's fine, as long as he doesn't get in the way of work. He understands that, being a man who worked most of his life, a man who understands the importance of work. But he's done his work. He's put in his time. And when he stopped to think about how he would like to spend his retirement, where he would like to spend his time, he realized he wanted to be with Amish.

Leaving.

THE WISE IS FREQUENTLY THE OBVIOUS. Where it is not the obvious it is upsetting. I usually go for the dramatic and try to think of something wise to say. But who am I kidding? I have nothing wise to say (not quite true, after all, I do have my pride), at least nothing exceedingly trenchant. It is all I can do to accurately describe the mundane. It is the slow, patient unraveling of the quotidian, the miracle of the regular that I am trying to do justice to. Anyway, wisdom is overvalued. We pay lip service to it but there is not much call for it. I only mention this because at some point in meanderings of this sort one is expected to come up with some sort of wisdom. It "rounds a work off." Ah, but this work is square and chunky, stubby, full of splinters, this little house I am building.

Our last day up here Harlow kept creeping closer and closer until he was squatting on the ridge just behind the house, the one with the silent oak that served as a line tree. I was busy with the details that go with leaving a house that is not quite built for the winter. Ladders to put away, tools to put back, instructions to the bulldozer man. The nails that must go in at the last minute. Holes covered, lumber put away. It seems like I've done this before, and I have. I've been putting things away for several days running, as if there is never enough to put away, or as if it is the putting away of things that I want to continue, that I want never to stop. I look at tools, touch them, do not want to put them away because I know there are many things I've forgotten, if only I could remember what it is I've forgotten. Carry the hammers in the car in case I'm going down the road at fifty or sixty and I see a nail that must be pounded in. Or a board just aching to be sawed.

The deep red of the roof against the hard blue of the sky. Timbers now covered with plywood. Dried mud on the floor. The sharp green grass against the dirty gold of the plywood. In a month that green will be gone. The colors will be gray and white. Even the gold of the wood inside the house will be paled by the light from reflecting snow, making the timbers look ghostlike, a paleness brushed with cold. There is something I want to say to Harlow but I do not know what it is. I don't know if he expects me to say anything, if he just wants me to be quiet, to be oblivious to him sitting there yards away or if I should take notice, smile, and nod. Not knowing this I do nothing except what I have been doing before.

Winter hurricane.

W E COME BACK several months later, chased upstate by the most vicious winter storm the East Coast has seen in a century. Frightened by the weather forecasts, the grocery stores in the morning are clogged with people who expect to be snowbound. By late morning a few flakes appear, and by early afternoon we get a proper introduction. The wind picks up, the sky grays, stiffens, and starts to swirl with snow. Late afternoon and early night the storm is here. Fists of snow lash out at the house we are staying in. There is a vicious wind from the northwest. The blizzard tumbles from the sky, a rush of ice and wind. It drives into the tiniest crack. All night we are battered. Despite the intensity of the wind, the snow produces an eerie silence. We turn on lights and look outside. We can barely see the night. Swirling powder. The storm has plunged us into a cloudy nest. New hills and valleys of white are woven around the house. Icy crystals punished by wind, restlessly moved, blown, drifted, driven.

Morning. A gray white cloud of ice is falling. No one goes out. At noon, as if by signal, the snow stops, the skies clear, but the wind keeps its heavy engines in gear. We are treated to a silent, sunny, white-whipped land, the ground sculpted, thick and soft.

We set off on skis down the road to the house. The red roof has not a speck of snow, the porch roof just a patch on the edge where the sun hasn't rested long enough. A crust of ice covers the snow around the house. Inside, the wind has blown the snow everywhere. Cold snow is curled in corners, blown into the cardboard cartons that hold the windows. We brush, shovel, push it out. Outside, on skis, we make our way up to the ridge and look across the meadow below us to the house. The wind does its best to discourage us from being there. The tips of my ears, nose, forehead seem to disappear. I cannot account for much feeling there. We ski into the woods where the wind is muted. And warmed up by activity and a well-tempered wind, we ski out again and down to the house. The sun has melted the snow we left on the porch. We nail more boards over the windows. It is freezing but I can feel warmth in the house. The wood has a great, frozen, golden glow to it. Spring is coming. Spring. We hope to put the windows and doors on, get all the trim and siding on. We hope. Spring is coming. But winter is still here. There is a bulge in the center of the floor. Uh oh.

Flowers and swamp.

THE GRAVEL DRIVEWAY that curves from the road to our little house needs a sluice. We have not yet put one in. Now it's June. The snow was heavy in late winter and the spring rains were abundant. As I dip down the driveway, to the right there is water, which should have been drained away by the yet-to-be-put-in sluice. A stand of purple iris pokes their blooms above the black water. Tiny tadpoles wiggle along the edges of the shore searching for mosquito larvae. Frogs may be sparse in other parts of the country. Not here. A large box turtle stares at me. If I had the sluice I might not have to worry about this water, but I can see what I would be missing.

The bulge in the floor is gone.

Cut into the beams? Are you crazy?

THE SECOND FLOOR HAS TO BE PUT ON and so a decision must be made about the joists for the second floor. The joists can be placed over the beams. This however gives us unnecessary space below, unusable space in fact, plus it reduces the headroom in the second floor by the thickness of the joists. Joist hangers can be used, steel pockets which are fastened to the beams. Structurally this is not a bad solution, and it leaves the joists level with the beams so space is not wasted. But it is ugly! Galvanized steel, shiny steel hangers, nailed into the wood for every joist seems like a violation. It is not pleasant to look at, and downstairs one spends a lot of time looking at the ceiling.

A third solution is to cut into the beams—to mortise and tenon the joists. But oh! Cut into those beams? Into that wood? The decision must be made the next day. I sleep fitfully that night, commiserating with the beams. But by the next morning I know that this is what must be done.

The joists are 4-by-6. Strictly speaking, these will not be mortise-and-tenon joints because the full end of the joist will be used—no tongue will be carved out of the joist to stick in

Hammer. Nail. Wood.

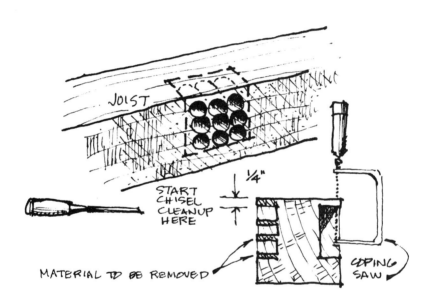

JOIST

START
CHISEL
CLEANUP
HERE

¼"

MATERIAL TO BE REMOVED

COPING
SAW

154

the beam. The mortise cuts will be one inch deep, 4"-by-6"-by-1". There will be six joists across, thirty inches apart, so six cuts will be made in either side of each beam, except on the end beams, which will only be cut on the inward-facing side.

Now you ask, these joists span nearly ten feet across and you're holding each end with one measly inch? Plus, wood shrinks, so in all probability the penetration will be less. Shouldn't the mortises be cut deeper? Perhaps, but I couldn't bear to cut any deeper into the beams, and, even allowing for shrinkage, the joists should still have enough length to be wedged solidly in place.

Remember now—four bents, which gives us three bays, six joists per bay, eighteen joists in all, so thirty-six cuts in the beams. The cuts are pencil scribed, holes are drilled to establish the one-inch depth and ease the hammer and chisel work, and then the fun begins.

I quickly learn not to start the chisel from the top side of the beam, but a quarter-inch or so below. The reason for this becomes apparent. If you make your cut from the top, the wood fibers on top tend to pull out, leaving a gouge there. But if you place the chisel just under the top side of the beam and work, the wood fibers are held in compression and tend to cut evenly and smoothly. When everything else is cut out you take a coping saw and make a clean cut to the top, establishing a neat slot for the joist.

This is not assembly-line work. The sides of the cut must be parallel, or as nearly parallel as possible, and also perpendicular to the top of the beam. The bottom cut should be flat and parallel to the top of the beam. The back of the cut must be flat and even, like the sides and bottom. It should be a snug fit. With the ends of the joist chamfered for ease of entry, the joist must nevertheless fit snugly into the slot, so snugly that it will need to be pounded into place, not with a hammer, which

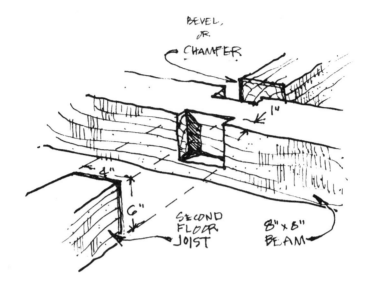

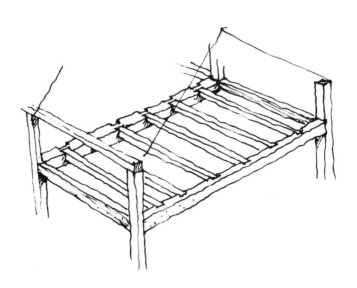

would mark up the wood, but with a mallet, neoprene if you are using a modern one or wood if you are lucky enough to get your hands on an old mallet.

Each joist has to be measured precisely for length, to be sure that there is not more than a sixteenth-of-an-inch variation over the course of an almost-ten-foot run. One very quickly learns after much pounding of joists in slots what is the proper degree of snugness—not so tight that it moves, not so loose that the joist is in danger of coming out.

Like baby bear's porridge, it must be just right.

After the joists are in place the subfloor is nailed on. The better surface of the boards face down. That is the side you will see. Then over the subfloor goes plywood. The plywood is both nailed and screwed, nailed where it crosses a joist or beam, screwed where it is only over subfloor.

Then you walk, run, stomp on the floor to see how solid it is. This one is.

Windows, doors, mistakes.

Except for some windows framed the wrong size, and except for some poor choices on some of the window dimensions, and except for corner casement windows across from one another with different widths, and except for the fact that I have not allowed for enough kitchen windows and must buy two new windows and then frame out for them, the windows and doors go in rather quickly and relatively easily. The mistakes are correctable, except for the wrong window size, and it is easier to just swallow that mistake. The slight difference in dimensions is not worth buying new windows. This is, after all, a budget job

It is a joy seeing the windows and doors in. The doors are glass, glass with a strong wood frame. The little house welcomes the light, and so do I.

Ants.

An ANT TRAIL RUNNING UP THE POST, across the beam. I am terrified. Sometime in the middle of the night, when I'm sleeping, they will carry the house away and I'll wake up in the cellar. Carpenter ants! Termites! They're going to eat my house up. How can you explain to ants that you don't want them to do that, that you will gladly supply them with other wood, that you will keep them supplied with all the wood they want as long as they don't eat your house? But ants are successful because they do not listen to you, never will. They do not care what you want. Beavers are the same way. The beaver dam I kept wrecking every morning one summer was always put back in the evening by the beavers. They don't care what you want.

Someone who knows more about ants than I do looks at the ants and tells me they're not termites and they're not carpenter ants. They are just plain ants. Attacking them with sprays, hammers, the palm of the hand does no good. After several days I realize why they are there.

They're just curious. Ants love houses, love wood. They are

Hammer. Nail. Wood.

there to see what's up, what gives, to suck resin. Ants are the
social butterflies of the insect world. They simply cannot keep
a secret. This is an ant house-warming.

The Amish visit.

SUNDAY IS VISITING TIME for the Amish. After church the buggy of the Amish family who lives down the road, thirteen children, stops by for a visit. The older children hop off the buggy before it turns in the driveway and run home. Their idea of a good time does not include visiting any "English" or "Gay" people, as non-Amish are called. Mose Miller (not to be confused with the Mose Miller who worked for me several months earlier) and his wife pull up to the house with five of their younger children. He ties his horse to the porch post and they come in. The children are dressed in stiff, starched clothes. They are barefoot, because this is summer. Knowing that they are coming we've bought ice cream. For the children, this makes the visit worthwhile. They eagerly, politely accept bowls of vanilla ice cream. One of the boys, five years old, is a dwarf and looks the size of a three-year-old. The children have straw-colored hair and large open eyes. It looks as if someone has rubbed rouge into their cheeks. Their skin is the color of cream. My wife and Mose's wife talk. Mose and I do little talking. Out on the porch he overestimates my age. The horse has left some manure we can use in the new garden.

Nails.

YOU DO NOT BUILD A HOUSE with screws or glue. You build a house with nails. Even a post-and-beam house, after the bents and bays have been pegged together, uses nails. I can hear someone screaming, "What about the sheetrock? What about the plywood on the floor? What about . . . ?" Sure, you use some screws, and you use some glue, but the main job of holding a house together is assigned to the lowly nail.

Get to know nails. They are your friends. They hold just about anything, and everything, together. During the course of building a house you will pound thousands of nails. You will ache in unfamiliar places, surprised by the muscles you use.

I would venture a guess that the nail is more important than the wheel, and that the man, woman, child who invented the first nail did more for civilization than with any other invention. Look at it this way. How could you invent the nail without inventing the hammer? And is there anything in the world as satisfying as pounding nails solidly into wood, feeling the great inner strength of wood with every blow of the hammer?

Nails are caressed into wood. Put a brick nail in mortar or concrete, and it must be pounded in. But a nail slips into wood. It shoots off the edge of the hammer and flies into the wood. A good nail man takes two or three hits to drive a nail into wood. He or she can feel the nail entering into the wood, and it is one of the most solid experiences one can have. The hammer head never hits the wood. The last hit conveniently drives the nail slightly below the surface. Conversely, driving a nail and missing the second or third piece of wood underneath, the anchoring layers, or missing the head of the nail and gouging the wood, is awful. You feel as if you have sacrificed lumber for no reason.

Nails are as varied as beetles, and they can bite just as hard. At one time they were made by the blacksmith. Each nail was slightly different, but they all had the characteristic wedge shape that the blacksmith's hammer produced. Some are still made this way for historic restoration projects.

Today nails are made in nail machines. I have never seen one of these machines, but it must be a huge, steel-gobbling piece of equipment. These machines are scattered all over the globe, in every country except the United States. Go to the hardware store and look where nails come from. Poland, Turkey, Taiwan, Japan, Yugoslavia (when there was such a country), India, Canada, and China are just a few of the countries that make them. A box of 6d's I saw had printed on the side in huge letters, PACKAGED WITH PRIDE IN THE USA and then in much smaller type, MADE IN CANADA. Oh well. I guess under the new economics we are all supposed to work making big Macs.

You may be kicked out of the hardware store, but I suggest going in and opening as many boxes of nails as you can. Grab a bunch and let them run through your fingers. You're holding one of the few marvelous things in the world that are cheap.

Buy all the nails you can. You never know when you'll need a nail. Say a 2-inch 6d galvanized box nail for siding, or a 3½-

inch 16d finish nail, or one of those great heavy, evil-looking 5-inch 40d ring-shank pole-barn oil-quenched nails (made, can you believe it, in the USA!). Maybe your taste runs to a 10d box galvanized, or a number 4 spiral standard, or a 3-inch common 10d, or a 16d coated box. How about a penny weight: 0 galvanized roofing 1-inch, 4d ring-shank dry-wall 1½-inch, 6d Ardox spiral concrete 2-inch, 8d finish 2½-inch, 10d common 3-inch, 16d Ardox galvanized deck 3½-inch.

In addition to the above, I also have: ring-shank dry-wall 1⅜-inch and 1⅝-inch, ring-shank underlay 1¼-inch and 2-inch, Ardox galvanized siding 8d and 10d, Ardox galvanized deck 16d, plus sinkers 6d, 8d, 16d, and finish 4d, 6d, 8d, plus galvanized roofing 1-inch, 1½-inch, 2-inch.

It takes at least twenty-five different kinds of nails to build a house, and I may be underestimating.

Suggestion. Do not try to reuse a bent nail. Unless you know your way around a hammer, and even then, toss the bent nail in your metal recycling bin (you do have one, don't you?). I know there are worse sights in the world, but I cringe every time I see a nail bent over on itself so only half of it is nailed into the wood. Seeing the end doubled over, lying alongside itself, the head pounded perpendicular into the wood, looks obscene, immoral.

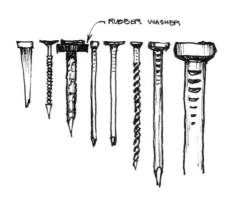

Plumbing and electricity.

THIS IS A LITTLE HOUSE so we will have as little plumbing and as much electricity as we can. The drains are plastic, hacksawed and glued. The kitchen is just opposite the near side of the septic system so it's a straight run down. But it needn't be. Water doesn't mind turning corners. The bathroom and shower are next to the kitchen. The biggest problem will be draining the system so it doesn't freeze in the winter.

Electric is running some wires from the entry box down to the crawl space and tacking them on the beam that runs down the center of the little house and then tacking them along the joists until you reach the spot where you want an outlet. Drill a hole, poke your wires through, attach it to the outlet box, and nail to stud. Bammo. Electric.

The next building, next door.

THIS ONE IS NOT FINISHED YET and I'm already thinking about where I'm going to store all the stuff, the ladders and table saws and canoes and anvils and so on, and I'm thinking about a small garage, something discrete, though maybe a little bigger, maybe not so discreet. I've got a lot of stuff. Something not as big as the little house, something simple, something I can put up in a couple of days, on pole foundations, gravel floor, a place to hold the car in really bad weather, a place to do all the repair work, with a workbench, a spot for tools, overhead rafters to store spare wood and construction equipment. You can't leave all that stuff outside. Absolutely impossible. I see something simple, no insulation, not much anyway, a few windows, garage doors, lower than the little house. Hell I can knock it together myself, in a few days, maybe with a little help, but I won't need much. It will be easy. Sure enough.

Ha!

How many boards go where the roof meets the side?

SEVEN OR EIGHT. Seven or eight separate boards that must be nailed all around the house, where the roof meets the side of the house. Fascia, trim board, nailers, boards to box in the eaves, signature board . . . and so on. Putting on the siding is a snap compared to putting on these boards.

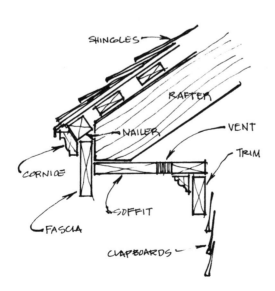

SHINGLES

RAFTER

NAILER

VENT

TRIM

CORNICE

SOFFIT

FASCIA

CLAPBOARDS

Small house, tall room.

I**F YOU MUST HAVE A SMALL HOUSE**, have tall ceilings. Cheap refrigerator and stove? Then buy good windows. Second-hand sink? Use first-rate lumber to hold the sink. Balance is all.

There is something disgusting about a house that has the best of everything, the most expensive. That house will overwhelm you. While in the first flush a new owner may revel in the forty-foot cathedral ceilings, marble floors, redwood decks, and ten-thousand-dollar stoves, in the longer run, say after the first year, a terrible depression will set in. You begin to realize that the house is better than you are, is more magnificent and more deserving than you could ever hope to be. If you don't come to this realization then quite frankly you are a bit stupid and somewhat insensitive and wander through life in a fog of ego. And I can't imagine why you are bothering to read this book.

This book, this house, and my life are about celebration and sorrow. The mistakes I have made in my life are for the most part mundane: a certain meanness, a lack of vision and spirit, flawed foresight. I have shown less courage than I should have. These are reflected in the house. And in these words. Indeed with these words, this book, unlike the house, I have had the luxury of a most extravagant budget. You see the result.

There is no apology for a cheap house. None is needed. A mobile home, a shack, is simply what it is and reflects the resources of the owner. There is no need to be ashamed of this even though our culture tries to shame us precisely for this. It tries to make us cringe because of our low-paying jobs, our modest circumstances. It succeeds more often than not.

What mortally wounds a cheap house is lack of spirit. It needs a touch of extravagance, a daring, a necessity missing and in its place a bold luxury, however minor that luxury may be. The expensive house lacks spirit because it desperately tries to buy spirit at any price, however outrageous, and knows it can't. An expensive house is hollow at the core because you can't buy spirit, and the house knows this and begins to look pathetic, all the rich, expensive objects cringing with shame. The cheap house will often lack spirit because the owner has been conditioned to live a life of shame, and as a result has nothing in his or her house that is out of the ordinary, that is not expected, not outrageous.

One of the most enjoyable houses I was ever in was a mobile home with the engine block from a Buick, a V-8, in the living room. This was being used as a table. With the cylinder heads pulled off, the holes for pistons made ideal caches for food and drink. Plus, that damn engine looked so good I couldn't imagine anything better there.

And anyway, what the hell are we supposed to do with our lives? Stand around and wait for someone to approve what we put in our house?

All he really wanted

was some work. He wanted me to hire him so he could pay his rent and put some gas in his motorcycle. But he wouldn't come out and ask me. He'd starve before he'd ask.

Harlow's in his late fifties. Fought the oreo war, the one in the middle, the one everyone forgot, the one between the Second World War and the Vietnam War. Those were the big wars, the first because it was heroic, a good war, and the second because it wasn't. What the hell was the Korean War anyway?

Harlow has worked in the rolling mills before they went out of business, in the lumber mills before Canadian lumber put him out of work, on his father's farm before his father sold that and pissed away the money. He's worked as an auto mechanic, on a road crew, grinding drum brakes, hauling junk for Emile and Skyler. He's done other things.

But he's getting close to sixty and he doesn't want to explain this. It goes beyond doesn't want. Will not.

He's willing to work. He wants to work. He needs to work. But he will not crawl to work. He will not beg.

Nobody wants him, that's the shameful truth.

They won't even hire him at McDonald's. He looks too rough. Didn't seem to bother the army any when they needed men to stop the Chinese from crossing the 38th parallel. That was probably the best job he ever had. They needed him then.

Well, what the hell . . . why doesn't he shave more often? How come he looks at you like he wants to crush you? Why doesn't he ever talk about the weather? Or sports? Why doesn't he talk?

("He gives me the creeps. I heard what he did to that motor vehicle man.")

He's good in the woods. He's handy with a chain saw. He can operate a backhoe. He's reasonable around vehicles. He knows how to grow vegetables. He doesn't whine. He's not destitute. He may be hungry but he's not starving. He'll get along. But he'd like a job.

His ex-wife doesn't want to see him anymore. And his son? Well . . .

Used to be you could always get a factory job. They weren't particular about you as long as you did the work, and did it well. Harlow could always do the work, but when people get particular about him, then it doesn't work. And neither does he.

All those factory jobs are gone. Those that are left want women, want young men, want someone who looks smooth.

Harlow's just a damn Korean War vet. But don't feel sorry for him or he'll put a fist in your face.

Women survive.

Donald's widow lived in the farmhouse with her daughter and husband who was on disability and their four kids who sat around the kitchen table all day eating frosted flakes and sugar buns. They put in a new well so the house could have running water and tore down some inside walls and put up insulation and then she decided to sell. Her daughter and her husband and their kids moved back to Gouverneur, and she moved somewhere else and waited while her lawyers tried to make sense out of her deed.

Skyler's widow dropped in at Dot's to have a drink and watch the men arm wrestle. Everyone in the place always had a story about Skyler and would insist she listen while they went on to bore her silly, until she had to decide between her social life and tales about Skyler. Finally she had a little card printed up. I DON'T WANT TO HEAR IT ANYMORE is what the card said, and by and large it worked.

Turned out a lot of people missed Skyler's junkyard. You could go over to Emile's but his place was all uphill, and the stuff he had was a different kind of junk. Hard to explain how junk can be different, but Skyler had more of the dangerous stuff, industrial stuff. The weather seemed to be better over at Skyler's too. Don't ask me how.

They wanted to hold a memorial service for Skyler but his widow said absolutely not. Skyler would not approve.

Emile's junkyard made a pigsty look antiseptic, but Em, Emile's wife, kept the cleanest kitchen on the face of the earth. Ever since the devil stopped chasing her while she was driving the school bus she kept busy driving the Wicked One out of her kitchen. Dirt was her enemy. Emile was a walking compost pile, so every time he came in the kitchen she had broom, dust pan, mop, bucket, soap, and water at the ready. She took his dirty plate and simply drove the scraps down the drain. Her kitchen had the cleanest cracked linoleum I have ever seen. Brain surgery could be performed on her kitchen table with no danger of infection.

Hot, she kept the kitchen hot. Even on the coldest day in winter you'd sweat in her kitchen, but you knew that your sweat would never reach the floor, or if it did, would be scoured clean in seconds. There would simply be no trace that you had sweated in that kitchen.

All because Em was on a new mission. She was going to bust that dirt, drive the devil out of that unclean.

Em was at White's Lumber in Canton getting some 1-bys when one of those "God-willing, the Lord-willing" women came in. They can't do anything without asking God for help. They're always praying for God's help to make lots of money and somehow have the idea that it is God's personal and overriding concern to make them rich, or at least well-off. Now no one is more devout than Em, but this just turned her stomach. Finally when the woman was going on about how her sewing machine kept dropping a stitch until she asked Our Personal Redeemer to intercede for her, and then she said, "Do you know what happened?"

"You had it threaded wrong," said Em, who added, "and would you please, for heaven's sake, just shut up."

Remember that bee woman who lived with Harlow for a while? She went kind of funny on us. She lived on bee pollen and herbs and never washed, herself or her clothes. She liked to climb on roofs at night and sing and sometimes walked down the highway buck naked holding a ginseng root. Finally she stopped when someone told her about the stuff they put in headlights to make them so bright.

She took to crying and mumbling to herself and eating chamomile. She put honey in jars and several people bought them. The jars were sticky and frequently the honey had bark or twigs in it, sometimes wax. But it was good honey. She cleaned up the glass and sold a few more jars. She could never be persuaded to put labels on the jars, but people knew where she lived and came out to buy her honey.

That made her feel good. She washed herself and her clothes. See what selling a little honey can do?

Most folks around here will take minimum wage for doing just about anything. Especially the women. Betsy worked in a factory, an unheated shed really, assembling air-conditioning ducts for minimum. Three hours of each day paid for her food. That left five hours for rent, utilities, clothes, and so on. She cut her hands assembling those ducts and had to miss work a week. Docked a week's wages. Took her a week to pay off the medical. Company wouldn't pay. And she works, so no Medicare.

Betsy doesn't complain. She's about five foot five and weighs two-forty-five. Her husband is out of work. Two children. Oh well, she says.

Worked. She doesn't work there anymore. Factory closed down and left town the day she learned she didn't have a job anymore. It was no problem. The town said they were glad to have the company, for however long. The state would clean up the toxic, the town thought.

But Betsy was lucky. She got a job as a waitress. All that money! "Honey," she said to her husband, "now I don't care if you ever find work." He didn't quite see it that way. He was laid off at the aluminum plant on the Seaway. "Jobs like that will never come back," he said. "That was triple, sometimes quadruple minimum wage. You'll never see jobs like that here, never again."

Shirley quickly disabused Betsy of the idea she would make a lot of money as a waitress. "Plus," Shirley said, "men come in and do really disgusting things with their food. Makes you want to vomit."

Eldon.

ELDON'S SPIRIT STILL HANGS over this place, over this land. He was a night watchman at a window-shade plant for twenty, thirty years. And he took home all those little parts that go into a window shade, the little spring-wound spools that roll up, the tiny, square steel caps, the round steel-cupped ends, cords, rings, window shades. He took it all home and kept it. He didn't have a window shade in his house. Not a curtain. He kept all that stuff stashed around, and when the Zooks bought his place I wondered where all that window shade stuff went. Then several years ago it began to turn up at auctions, at flea markets. It was always with a box of something else, baseball cards or old fuses, fishing hooks or faucet washers. People would bid for the other and end up with some of Eldon's window-shade stuff. And I wonder if he was saving it up for just this time, years after he saved it, when someone would come upon some string or rings with fabric around them or small, square steel bars that fit on the end of window-shade spools and would wonder, what was this . . . what did this do? And Eldon would say, "If I was around I would tell you. I would tell you exactly what they did."

1953 Allis Chalmers, 1965 Ford 150, 1968 Dodge Slant Six.

I F   Y O U   W A N T   T O   B U Y   A   V E H I C L E with an internal combustion engine that will last, you buy American and you buy something built before 1970. All the American cars and trucks started going to hell in the 1970s. Some people say it was when they let hippies on the assembly line and some people say it was when they let accountants and Wall Street people run the car companies, but whatever it was, it would be hard to find an American car or truck built in the 1970s that's worth a pig's foot, except for International Harvester trucks (and tractors), and they're out of business now.

I hear they make cars and trucks better today, especially in this country, but you can't kill an old Dodge Slant Six, except with a bazooka, and the same goes for an old Ford six-cylinder pickup truck. Allis-Chalmers is one of the sweetest tractors ever made. You can still find many of them plowing and pulling but you can't go into a showroom and buy one because they're out of business. I know someone who gave up a new table saw for an old DeWalt table saw, made in Lancaster, Pennsylvania. DeWalt was bought up by Black & Decker and the first thing they did was to close up the plant in

Lancaster and discontinue the line. Then, oddity of oddities, they kept hearing from old-time carpenters how great DeWalt power tools were, so they revived the line. Now they're built in Maryland. I have no idea how good they are now, or if they match up to Milwaukee power tools.

It's easy to develop nostalgia for old machines. Many of them were not as good as the stuff they're making today. But there were a few . . . oh, they were special.

Siding, stain, ladders, scaffolds.

Vinyl siding is cheaper, never needs painting, always looks the same, and from a distance, say beyond ten feet, you can't tell the difference. I decide to put on wood siding. White pine. Thin stuff. You can't let it get wet before you put it on, and after you nail it on you better stain it quickly and then do the same thing in a year and then ten years later. It curls, it warps, it twists. It does provide a shade more insulation than vinyl and a bit more structural rigidity.

Ladders and scaffolding become crucial, especially for a building this size. You want a well-made ladder. You want to be very careful about how you put the ladder up. You want to make sure the top and bottom of the ladder are firmly placed. Be stable before you get up. After, twenty, thirty feet up, it's too late. A decal on the side of the ladder will show you the proper angle between the ladder and the building.

The stain goes on, a color no one up here has ever seen. They say the place looks like an army barracks, or a battleship.

Filling the place with junk.

So AFTER THE SECOND FLOOR GOES ON and the plywood gets nailed on over the joists and beams and screwed on over the floorboards, and the beautiful glass French doors and glass front door are opened, along with the breathtaking windows that let in a gorgeous sweep of meadow and the hills beyond and the pine and hemlock and maple in the distance, and after the afternoon sun burnishes the beams with a tawny apricot glow, set off by the sparkling wood-white of the second floor joists, 4-by-6 hemlock, and the hemlock floorboards above, after this, we bring in the junk.

Junk is different than stuff. Stuff is newer. Stuff can do stuff, and though junk can also do stuff, it did it so long ago that now it is doubtful if it can do the same stuff or do it as well as it used to. Junk can be cheaper or more expensive. Junk is stuff gone to pot. The charm of junk is that it once could have been used. It is the nostalgia of that long-gone use that charms, fascinates.

All this junk has been stored in the barn until we found a place to put it. An old trunk with the bottom falling out. A leather jacket with silver-dollar-sized mold rings. A round, empty, mouse-eaten Mother's Oats box, ravaged beyond re-pair, with the qualities of this breakfast cereal extolled on the side. A rusty beam borer, just like the rusty one I bought and needn't have bought if I had only known I had this one. Knives, forks, and spoons blended together in one Ur glop of metal rust. Nibbled on baseball cards. A mouse nest of a catcher's mitt. All junk. Blotted poems. Questionable junk.

More. Metal and wood in various stages of decay. Broken glass, with its spidery thinness and wicked flesh-catching edges. Patches of lace, linen blankets with holes in them, old quilts torn and stained. Thin pots with holes in the bottom. Deep-rusted iron skillets. An old apple-peeler whose edge is too moonbeam-thin to sharpen.

Sixty-eight pounds of this we toss out, and we pay for the privilege in this new age of recycling centers. The rest we carry upstairs and stack on the new floor, on the new wood, under the new roof, where we can sit and look at it and watch it de-cay. This is not the way to deal with junk.

You go out and buy more junk. We probably will. But junk does not have to be looked at. You should stack it somewhere off to the side, hidden, in its own room, a separate closet.

Stuff has to be out on view. You have to be able to see stuff, otherwise, it's hardly stuff. Stuff can still do stuff, but you hardly want it to. Do you really want to wash yourself with that teeny soap bar from Motel 8? Or set your drink on a plas-tic coaster from the Dew Drop Inn?

You can tell the difference between a junk collector and a stuff collector. The one is a consumer: eager, impatient, al-most fretful. The other lingers, turns the object over, feels its heft. They can drive the same cars, wear the same clothes, but as soon as they get out of the car, you can spot junk from stuff. Sometimes, though rarely, they battle for the same . . . "things."

Canada, Old DeKalb, and the Junction.

Donald lived twenty miles from Canada. He never got there. He never wanted to. Eldon worked in Ogdensburg and confined his travels between the window-shade factory and his farm. He was a night watchman so he spent most of his days sleeping and feeding the huge wood stove that sat in his living room and setting out food for the cats. Irma is in her early twenties. She lives in the Junction, on welfare. She likes to sing in the early morning, two or three A.M., on the porch roof. She has a baby, courtesy of one of the workers brought in to lay the gas line that comes up from the Southwest. It was a southern company that paid their workers well. The men in their turn liked to have a good time, and so did Irma, and she did, and now they're gone and she has a cute blond baby. She fondly remembers the good times. She wouldn't think of leaving the Junction.

The little house is twenty miles from Canada, one mile from Old Dekalb, and another five from Dekalb Junction. The big two-lane highway is Rt. 11. The Junction is on that, and the pipeline runs along the highway. Scattered along Rt. 11 are farms, truckstops, a John Deere Dealer, a few diners, marsh, and the railroad tracks.

Shirley is on Rt. 11, her diner is. She lives in Canton over Merrill Bros. Hardware, an old-time hardware store that survived the influx of the chains by going into the sheet-metal business. Shirley was set to leave. Had enough of this small time and planned to move to Ithaca or Rome, doing what she didn't know, maybe a job in an office where she wasn't around grease all day. She was planning to leave any day. She was tired of Harlow and his moods and men like him, heavy men, gruff and demanding, who thought nothing of grabbing you or spitting on their plates (those were the polite ones).

Any day now.

She hates working and she hates being home alone and she hates the choice of men she has to bring home so she doesn't bring anyone home, hardly anyone. Shirley is a big woman, not fat, big-boned, good breasts, firm shoulders, strong in the legs and hips. Being strong has helped her get out of trouble. She does a little drinking, but not much, has a little sex, but not much, and spends most of her time wishing she were somewhere else. But when she stops to imagine what she would like to be doing somewhere else, nothing comes to mind. "Goddamn," she says. She cries a little, but not much. "What the hell is it?" she asks herself. "What the hell is it all about?"

She visits a married sister in Albany. Her sister's husband is a real jerk, not a phony jerk, but the real-McCoy asshole. Her sister told her. Her sister told her never to get married. Her sister said it was the biggest mistake she'd ever made. A kid. "I hate this child," the sister told her. "This girl is growing up to be just like my husband. There's nothing I can do about it." When Shirley told her to get divorced and get a job, the sister said she couldn't. "This is all I can do," she said, crying.

Hammer. Nail. Wood.

Shirley drove back to Canton thoroughly depressed. She laughed to herself because she knew she would never commit suicide. She was too depressed for that. Once she joined the Richville Methodist Church to meet . . . men? . . . someone? She couldn't even find God there. How pathetic! she thought. How goddamn pathetic can you get!

Sex. When she has sex it is gloomy sex. Pull down the pants, pull up the dress, back on the bed, go to the bathroom. She feels like a toilet. Lights on or lights off. Day or night. Where is the passion? She wants to be kissed, she wants to be fondled. She wants everything that happens before sex to have a sort of frantic majesty to it, a glowing majesty that goes on, an intense majesty that has a hint of the cabin by the river she remembered going to when she was young, with her parents, with no electricity and one toilet, where you could hear everything through the plywood walls and the trees seemed to drip with erotic fruit, and even the water rushing by in clear swirls and bubbles made her terribly excited. Where is that excitement now? With men it's like eating. They want to get it over with as soon as possible. Where is the joy?

OK, stop feeling sorry for yourself. She's good at catching herself when she gets maudlin, straightening herself out. Good strong German woman. Way she was brought up. But self-pity is a kind of pleasure. Can't we allow ourselves a bit of it? she thinks. Must we deny ourselves that pleasure too?

She imagines the smell of fresh pine dripped on by water. She imagines a wet afternoon, whitened by the damp, the cabin steamy and secluded by the river. She imagines a time before she knew about sex, that is, when she knew about it but was shy on the details. She imagines that time when she was eleven or twelve and got so terribly excited in her body she shook like a leaf. She would tremble, and her mother would find her and ask her what was wrong and she was embarrassed to tell her that nothing was wrong, that everything was terribly right. She imagines that river, that woods, the smell of the shellac on the cheap plywood counter that never quite dripped the water off, the electric bulb that bumped your head, the sag in the floor near the door, the damp wool blankets she and her sister were forced to use, and her parents, who never made a sound at night, who knew how thin the plywood was and did it in silence, the way she is doing it now.

The cabin collapsed, the land was sold. There is nothing sad about that.

Rome, Ithaca. That's a long way off. Donald never made it, nor Eldon.

Shirley looks out of her bedroom window to the buildings across the street. They are pretty much like hers. Three-story, brick. The trim is different. There's the *St. Lawrence Plain Dealer* newspaper, getting a lot of competition from a big midwestern chain of papers, then itself bought up by a chain. There's the pawn shop that went out of business and the Alcohol and Substance Abuse Center, and then a jump across the alley to a liquor store and further down a basement bar. On the corner is a department store, or what would be a department store, perhaps a discount store, or an Army–Navy store. It can't make up its mind what it is, which is academic anyway since it's going out of business. There's no bookstore, but there's an art gallery run by the wife of a professor of ceramic sculpture at St. Lawrence University. She sells prints, ceramics, and other crafts, Amish quilts. The university has a bookstore, mostly textbooks and a few bestsellers.

The name of the main street that runs through Canton is Main Street. Canton is brightened up and also boozed up by the University. Young drinkers learning how to drive while drunk. Noise and vomiting. A duplex movie theater. A new store opened that sells bagels and coffee in flavors. The only coffee flavor people up north know is bitter. Ten thousand people, close to half with a University connection. The Junction is one-fortieth that, but just as many bars and the people know how to drink and do their vomiting in the toilet. Old Dekalb is one-fifth of that: a bend in the road, D & L, the combination general store and gas station where you can get night crawlers, sugar pops, and you used to be able to get X-rated videos, and several houses.

Shirley's diner is near the Junction. The Agway at the town's one traffic light went out of business but the bar never did and the trucks still go by on their way from Plattsburgh to Watertown with hungry truckdrivers who need food. Shirley knows how to dish it out.

"Run away with me, baby," the truckers say.

"To Watertown?" she says. "To Plattsburgh?" she says. "You must be kidding."

Then Merrill Bros. Hardware went out of business and Shirley had to move. Don't ask me where she lives now.

Water, hot and cold.

THERE IS SOMETHING THAT SITS on top of the sink with a handle, two handles. Each handle is for a different temperature. The water pump is a noisy contraption that we bought used from the man who delivered the mail in his Dodge Slant Six. "Forty bucks if it works," he said. It did. He got his forty. We still use the outhouse because we haven't put in the bathroom yet because we ran out of money, but I say that hot and cold water just gushing out of the faucet over the sink fills my heart with joy. I don't even care if the drain leaks a bit in the basement. OK, I do, but it will get fixed.

What there is to a house is joy and heartache, and the two are enmeshed, like lovers in heat, thrashing their sex about in bed. If you want that thrash you got to take both.

Now I worry if the little house will make it through another winter. There's more to it than last winter, so it should be more protected, but there's also more to go wrong if something does go wrong. Well, I put love in that little house so I've got to take the heartache too.

The staining is just about complete, much of the caulking is done, the floor upstairs has been nailed and screw-gunned down. Next comes the wiring, then more studding and wiring, then the insulation, then some sheetrock.

I've got to wait for next year. Winter is coming. Next year. We all wait. Harlow, Shirley, Dot, even Eldon and Donald . . . we all wait.

Killer highway.

IN THE COLLEGE TOWN ten miles away they learn to drink but they do not learn to drive, and they certainly do not learn to drink and drive, but they do that anyway. At the Junction, Dekalb, Rt. 28 crosses Rt. 11. The latter is the big highway and the former shows its respect with a stop sign when it bumps into Rt. 11. You've got to build up speed pretty fast to be traveling seventy through the Junction headed south toward Rt. 11, because there's a wicked right-angle turn several hundred feet from the stop sign. But these four college kids had a brand-new car, a fast one, a new Oldsmobile, and the driver was pig-blind drunk, as were, probably, all his passengers. When he came to the stop sign there was no way in hell he was going to stop. There was no way he could stop. Not at seventy. He didn't even try, but sailed right across Rt. 11 and obliterated a family coming back from a movie. Seven or eight bodies all told. That's what they were. They never got beyond bodies. People could hardly believe metal could get so twisted.

Then there was the Army captain who wanted to commit suicide. He didn't have far to go. It was just a few steps into eternity. He stepped in front of a tractor-trailer truck. They call them semis in the city. Here they call them tractor-trailers. They make it sound like one word, but they don't miss a syllable, not a one. Someone saw him jump in front of this tractor-trailer going through the Junction at a modest sixty-five. The volunteer firemen had to clean him up. They said it was the worst thing they had ever done. They had to use a shovel to get him off the road. Somehow his head wasn't crushed, but neither was it with his body when they found it. And his two upraised hands, like ghosts, left their imprint on the fenders. Right there on the fenders you could see them. Couldn't even wash them off.

They said he was despondent. He had been retired from the Army. He couldn't find a job. He left a note, telling that. When they buried him they think they had most of him in the coffin.

Screened-in porch.

THE ONLY THING that beats a screened-in porch is a porch that is not screened in, and the only thing that beats that is a screened-in porch when the bugs are out. Now the toilet is in and we don't have to use the outhouse. I used to think how superior I was using the outhouse. What did I need a toilet for? Another stupid idea. Now I never use the outhouse, not when I can avoid it.

Last spring it was so wet the water bubbled up out of the well and we had to dig a channel to drain it off. There was a wildlife refuge by the side of the driveway near the road, where I vowed to put a sluice in to drain off the water, filled with purple iris, frogs, turtles, and swamp grass that waved at me in the wind as I went by. This spring it hasn't rained for a month. The pond by the driveway is no more, the earth dry and cracked where the pond was, changing color from a deep black to a dull gray as the drought has continued. Perhaps I won't put that sluice in, even if the water overflows the driveway during wet weather and I have to drive over a river.

Pristine nature lovers irritate me. Don't change nature, don't alter nature they shout, finishing up their vegetarian meal and wearing their non-animal-skin clothes. But nature changes nature, nature alters itself.

Animal lovers who castigate hunters have never seen a sea gull hunting baby chicks, or watched wolves pull down deer and start their dinner before the creature is dead. Nature is not polite. It just is. The planet is alive and bubbling inside, and once in a while spits up a bit of excess that has given it indigestion. It wears old clothes, feels a need to change them, splitting its mantle of rock and earth and shreds itself along fault lines. The weather disrupts lives and alters countries. Elephants, beavers, ants, one-celled organisms, and a host of other species, including human beings, can wreak havoc on the environment. But it is only human beings who have the capacity for shame, and the will to alter their course of action.

Nature is indifferent to what it becomes, so if we wish to live in a cess pool and breath toxic gases, nature will oblige.

What is natural?

From my front porch I sit looking at a half-hayed meadow. The unmowed hay ripples like the surface of a windy ocean, while the green and wondrous smell of fresh cut hay lies softly on the land. Two hundred years ago this was forest and swamp. I prefer the hay. That's not to say I want all hay, or wouldn't like the red oak back. Up on the ridge where the soil is rocky, and further back to the river the forest lies, and will stay if I have any vote in the matter.

But it is that mingling contrast between meadow and forest, hay and evergreens, it is those combined smells, sights, and sounds that beguiles the senses and delights the mind.

This home is as natural as an ant colony. In fact it may be an ant colony, if I cannot convince them to do their exploring elsewhere. The ants will probably prevail. I hope humans do.

While I have been building this house off and on for the last five years, the house has been building me.

Now I am concerned about the land around the house, cutting brush and planting trees. Now instead of fussing about the details of the house I am fussing about the details of the land.

It is more important that the land "feel" right, that it have comfortable shade trees of oak and maple, butternut trees for the birds, evergreens for wind protection, fruit trees, flowering crab apples, a majestic American beech, a dawn redwood (why not?), some black walnut up on the ridge.

We spend our money on trees instead of furniture—the sofa, easy chair, and several not-so-easy chairs we scrounged from the streets of New York City. I can feel as comfortable in an old ratty sofa as in one that costs as much as I paid for my used car. But when I look out the windows several years from now and see the sugar maples taking off, and the burr and pin oaks thriving, and birds leaving us a few berries from our new berry bushes—that is my comfort.

I, we, my wife and I, have done our best. Perhaps we have given something of value to this land by building this house . . . by saying, look, we want to take care of these acres.

We ask for blessing on this house, and our work.

CHELSEA GREEN

Sustainable living has many facets. Chelsea Green's celebration of the sustainable arts has led us to publish trend-setting books about organic gardening, solar electricity and renewable energy, innovative building techniques, regenerative forestry, local and bioregional democracy, and whole foods. The company's published works, while intensely practical, are also entertaining and inspirational, demonstrating that an ecological approach to life is consistent with producing beautiful, eloquent, and useful books, videos, and audio cassettes.

For more information about Chelsea Green, or to request a free catalog, call toll-free (800) 639-4099, or write to us at P.O. Box 428, White River Junction, Vermont 05001. Visit our Web site at www.chelseagreen.com.

Chelsea Green's titles include:

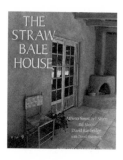 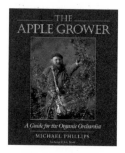 

The Straw Bale House
The Independent Home:
   Living Well with Power
   from the Sun, Wind,
   and Water
Independent Builder:
   Designing & Building a
   House Your Own Way
The Rammed Earth House
The Passive Solar House
The Sauna
Wind Power for Home &
   Business
The Solar Living Sourcebook
A Shelter Sketchbook
Mortgage-Free!
Hammer. Nail. Wood.

The Apple Grower
The Flower Farmer
Passport to Gardening:
   A Sourcebook for the
   21st-Century
The New Organic Grower
Four-Season Harvest
Solar Gardening
Straight-Ahead Organic
The Contrary Farmer
The Contrary Farmer's
   Invitation to Gardening
Forest Gardening
Whole Foods Companion
Simple Food for the
   Good Life
The Bread Builder

Gaviotas: A Village to
   Reinvent the World
Who Owns the Sun?
Global Spin:
   The Corporate Assault
   on Environmentalism
Hemp Horizons
A Patch of Eden
A Place in the Sun
Renewables Are Ready
Beyond the Limits
Loving and Leaving the
   Good Life
The Man Who Planted Trees
The Northern Forest
Scott Nearing: The Making
   of a Homesteader